BASED ON TRUE EVENTS

LITTLE YELLOW LIES

ON THE RUN EATING

Little Yellow Lies: On the Run Eating" by Ming the Merciless
Copyright © published in 2021 by: DiWulf Publishing House
ISBN 978-1-66781-340-0

Edited by Steven DiLodovico
Book Layout and Design by Orlando Arce
Cover art by Topaz

Ming. Watertown Correctional Facility 2002

Dedicated to Honey.

Thanks to everyone who helped me along on my journey, from immediate family to my close friends whom I consider family.

Chapter 1: Coming Home

I

Decisions. They craft who you are in life. When you become aware of your decisions, you begin making a conscious effort to change your habits and lifestyle. Starting this journey, you understand that change doesn't happen overnight. There are times when you might slip up and return to the same patterns and behaviors. There are false starts and, often, many stumbles along the way. There are times when you begin to feel like a prisoner of your past, where what you've done becomes who you are. There are times when life seems like a perpetual cycle of advancing two steps forward and five steps back. You question your personal growth. You question any and all change.

For Mike Lee, this change began while he was incarcerated. Mike spent the ages of 23 to 27 in several correctional facilities. Most of his time was done in Watertown Correctional Facility for armed robbery. His time there motivated him to find a new path and change his life.

Mike had spent a good amount of time in and out

of juvenile detention centers. Growing up Asian in the crime-polluted area of East New York (the murder capital of NYC), it seemed inevitable that he would eventually become a statistic. Mike was wild, there was no question about it. He was known and he had maneuvered his way through his perilous environment for years before being put away. Mike's violent ways were legendary in his neighborhood and his reputation was well-earned.

On the day of his release, Mike wore a Roca-Wear jumpsuit and a fresh pair of white Nike Uptowns. His wardrobe alone would not readily indicate that he had just been released from prison.

Mike was looking forward to seeing his sister, Amy, who was driving six hours upstate to bring him back home to Brooklyn. She was happy to see him, too, and remarked about how healthy he looked. She brought him up to date on everything that had gone on in her life while he was incarcerated. Life had become radically different for his family during his time away. His father used to own a business, now he was retired, and social security wasn't covering it. His mother was a stay-at-home-mom caring for his little brother. They were barely getting by. But, even with all this looming over the family, everyone was excited for him to come home and have a fresh start. The only thing on his mind was his next move: it had to be his best move.

As Mike and Amy walked to her car, Mike saw the balloons she had tied to the back, saying "welcome home" and it made him smile. Mike felt like he was on top of the world. He had a chance and it seemed promising. He had clung to it for so long on the inside that its arrival didn't seem real. He had to quickly shake the prison mindset and hit the ground running. He would have to start from scratch again, but he would not let the enormity of the task dissuade or demoralize him. Everything was before him right now, at this very moment, and his path was his own.

A six-hour drive back to Brooklyn would give him ample time to think about his new beginning. Brother and sister sat in silence for a minute, pausing to take stock of the moment while trying to find the right words. Before Mike could even open his mouth to ask Amy for advice, her phone rang.

"Hello?"

Mike could hear a muffled voice, but he couldn't make out the words. He glanced over at Amy and noticed a panicked expression on her face. He knew there was bad news on the other end of that conversation.

"*He's been what?*" Amy was screaming. Her face reddened and her eyes welled up with tears. She froze, completely speechless. She dropped her phone. They were both completely silent, the only sound being the low hum of the car's engine. With no warning, Amy began wailing on the steering wheel and kicking the floor. The engine revved furiously every time her foot would nip the side of the gas pedal. He knew his sister's capacity for explosive rage, and he waited for it to erupt.

Completely numbed by what she heard on the phone Amy started the car. Tears blinded her vision as she drove, speed increasing, recklessness and rage urging her onward. Mike was beginning to panic.

"Amy, what's going on? What's wrong?"

She was sobbing in exhaustion and defeat. The car slowed and she pulled to the side of the road. Mike reached over and snatched the keys out of the ignition.

"Are you okay? What's going on?" Amy kept sobbing, convulsing with emotion. She banged on the steering wheel again.

"My boyfriend has been shot," she screamed. He was at a loss. He had no idea how to respond. He felt his sister's pain.

They sat in silence for a while. Amy was balled up in the driver's seat, sobbing softly. Mike's heart was breaking for his sister, but he had to explain to her that there was nothing he could do. At first, she argued, but as she slowly regained her composure, she admitted she understood. She started the car and drove off.

"I'm glad you understand," said Mike.

Mike was firm in his decision to steer clear of

anything that could lead him in the wrong direction. He knew that if he went home, his sister would be a threat to his stability. He decided to stay at a shelter in Manhattan for the night. He could clear his head, think to himself, plan his next moves, and go see his parole officer in the morning. The parole officer was close to the shelter. He had no problem getting in the shelter. The prison had given him a state I.D. along with his release papers. The papers confirmed Mike's freedom, and they granted him access to any shelter within 72 hours of his release.

The shelter assigned Mike a room, but before he dropped his belongings off, he went to the cafeteria. The cafeteria reeked of bleach. The tables, chairs, and floors were drenched in it. The food looked like bad leftovers from some forgotten time. Mike got a plate of lukewarm, semi-solid baked beans, a thigh of chicken so dry that it looked like an archeological relic, and some limp, thawed-out frozen vegetables. The food was bland and flavorless like the shelter. It tasted like nothing. Literally nothing. Mike had lived through worse days in prison, so it didn't really faze him. He sat quietly alone and felt out of place.

The people at the shelter were homeless and unstable. Small pockets of residents stood talking among themselves while others sat alone talking and laughing out loud. Mike decided this would be his last night here, and he wouldn't make this his space for any longer than it needed to be. He became weary of the soft chaos of the cafeteria and went back to his room. Upon entering his room, he was confronted by the overwhelming stench of old urine. He went over and laid on his bed, which was a graham-cracker-thin piece of mattress under a sheet that was so threadbare it was nearly transparent. The walls were brick; cold and windowless. Despite all this, Mike had no complaints. He was used to this type of living. For three and a half years it had been his reality. So many thoughts were running through his head that falling asleep was impossible.

"*Get off me*! *Don't touch my shit*! *You don't know me*," a young man suddenly screamed from just outside the doorway. As the commotion got closer and louder, Mike lifted his head. His body tensed and he braced himself. He heard an authoritative voice say: "That's enough." Just as Mike was about to get up, one of the guards threw a scrawny man into his room and shut the door. Mike took a closer look at his new roommate. He wasn't old or crazy. He was just a skinny, young, Black boy, no older than 21, looking for a place to sleep. He didn't seem to be homeless, and his clothes weren't ragged. In fact, he had on the latest Jordans. Mike was totally confused by this and wondered why this young man was staying in a shelter.

"What happened out there?" asked Mike.

"This bum tried to take my shoes!" the boy said,

angrily. He was pouting, breathing heavily, and a thick vein was prominent, bulging visibly on his forehead. Mike realized this was the person who had been screaming outside his room.

"Yeah, man, those are definitely some nice shoes," Mike said, trying to lighten the mood. "Why are you here?" he asked.

The young man looked over at Mike and replied in exasperation: "Because I have nowhere to stay right now."

"Nowhere to stay? How do you have nowhere to stay? Look at your clothes, you don't look homeless at all."

"I usually stay with my grandma, but she kicked me out."

"Kicked you out for what?"

"Selling weed. That's how I get money."

Mike thought about the decisions he had made in his own life, and he felt moved to speak to the young man from a place of guidance.

"It's not worth it at all, you should listen to your grandmother. She knows what's right for you. Look at me, I'm just coming home from a three-and-a-half-year bid. I have absolutely nothing. I'm telling you from experience, the streets will only lead you two places."

"Dead or in prison," they said in unison.

"Yeah, yeah I know. My Grandma tells me all the

time."

"So, stop wasting time," Mike said. "Pick up a trade, get a real job."

Mike heard himself saying these words, his voice trying to adopt a fatherly, sagacious note and it sounded false. He was not there yet.

Mike needed to get a regular job himself so he could work his way up and better himself and make his money legally. He wasn't sure where he was going to work, but he would set modest goals for himself and go from there in as orderly and professionally a manner as possible.

II

The following morning, Mike woke up to an empty room. His young roommate was gone. He didn't think much of it. He went to the cafeteria for breakfast, and, as expected, the food was trash. He returned the room key to the front desk and promised himself he would never go back.

Mike's parole officer was a twenty-minute train ride away, an hour on foot. He didn't have any money. It was 9 a.m. and he didn't have to meet his parole officer until 11. This worked out perfectly because it gave him time to think. While walking, he passed McDonald's, Footlocker, and several other places he could work. He was willing to do anything and work anywhere. It felt strange. He wasn't familiar with asking for job applications. Being incarcerated didn't exactly help. He knew a lot of people didn't want to hire someone with a criminal record, and he knew he was going to have a tough time. He went to as many stores as possible. When filling out the paperwork, there was *always* the inevitable question: *Have you ever been convicted of a crime? If the answer is yes, please explain.* His first reaction was to lie, but beneath the question in big, bold letters were the ominous words: *Background checks are mandatory.* He didn't want to take any chances. He hoped that if he told the truth, the managers would overlook his past and understand that he was trying to turn his life around. He felt good about taking that first step. They said it would take about a week for a call back.

Mike was on time to meet his parole officer. He was ready to deliver the good news: In less than two days since his release he had already submitted applications. He was eager to show his P.O. he was willing to change. He was surprised to discover his new parole officer was a woman. Talking to women did not come easy to Mike, and she was very attractive. It was uncomfortable. He would freeze up and become tongue-tied. Having been surrounded by men during his bid changed the way he interacted with women.

"Ms. Hubbert?" Mike asked timidly, clearing his throat. "Hello, I'm Mike, Mike Lee." She was on a phone call, and without looking up from her computer screen she gestured toward the chair on the other side of the desk, ushering him to the seat.

"I'll be right with you. Thank you for being on time."

Mike sat. The chair was the most comfortable thing he had encountered in a long time. She seemed nice. She also seemed very stern and busy. She was scheduling future appointments with another parolee.

"I really can't stand this job sometimes," she said with an attitude. "I'm sorry for the hold up, how are you?"

In a low voice, Mike replied: "I'm good."

"I heard you say something about a job, tell me about that."

Before Mike could say anything, she went on a rant about how most people who get out of prison never try to do better for themselves. She went on about how the recidivism rate was so high because of how easily people fell right back into old ways. She claimed she had taken the job to help people. Mike was beginning to doubt that.

Mike responded with a smile. "I've been a free man for only a few days, and I've already found some places to apply." He was determined to not be a statistic.

Ms. Hubbert's usual clients often had no idea

what they wanted out of life. She replied: "That is very ambitious. This is a great start."

"I understand that a lot of life is simply patterns and habits. I'm making a conscious choice to change the way I think, and I am striving to keep my mindset positive. I'm also going to stay as productive as possible and create a whole new lifestyle, become a totally new person," Mike said, smiling, proud of himself.

Ms. Hubbert was astonished. "Just keep out of trouble and these next five years will be a breeze."

"I'm going to be coming here for the next five years?" Mike was confused.

"Yes," she said. "I will be your parole officer for the next five years."

Mike was shocked to learn the length of his parole. He wondered if he'd be able to keep out of trouble for five years. Ms. Hubbert gave him a breakdown of what he was allowed to do on parole, as well as different types of situations to avoid. He wasn't allowed to ingest substances of any kind. He would have random drug tests.

"You're going to see me once a week until I feel that we can space our meetings out some more, understand?" She had a serious look on her face.

"I got it," said Mike.

"When we meet next week let me know if anyone called you back. If not, don't be discouraged. There are opportunities out there. You have a good week, Mike. Stay positive and stay out of trouble."

On his way out, Mike calculated how long five years was: 1,825 days. 43,800 hours. For 43,800 hours, he would have to stay clear of any trouble. There had already been a shooting with his sister's boyfriend, and that was exactly the type of situation Mike needed to avoid.

They gave Mike a two-fare Metrocard to get home. The 3 train took him straight back to East New York, the belly of the beast. Nothing much had changed about public transportation. It was still dirty. Foul odors, rats on the tracks, scuttling putrid cockroaches, junkies nodding, and bums sleeping on train cars. When he reached his stop, he was anxious to see if anything was different about his neighborhood. He started to tense up, thinking about the last time he was here. This was the location of the crime that landed him in prison. Being here again brought up a lot of stressful memories. And, in a strange way, his once familiar and comforting surroundings made him feel sad. He couldn't figure out why. The entire time he was inside all he had thought about was home. It was the one place he should have felt safe. Instead, he just felt empty and unrecognized.

He needed to keep moving to distract himself, and to work off some of the anxiety. Instead of going straight home, he took a walk. It was a beautiful day. He took it all in, appreciating all the things he had taken for granted before he went to prison. The trees, the sky, buildings, hearing birds, cars, and trucks... just general city noise. Compared to the cold gray of prison, the world was so bright and colorful. The freedom felt amazing, he could feel it with every step. It was calming and euphoric. When Mike was in the prison courtyard, the only walking he did was in circles. The same scenery, the same faces, the same footsteps, day after day. Now, walking a straight path gave him some freedom, a destination, even. It was a metaphor for his current situation.

As he walked down the streets of his hometown, he noticed a lot of the same people doing a lot of the same things. There were very few differences: a few new stores had popped up, and some older ones had shut down. He couldn't remember the stores that had left.

After he walked the strip, Mike went to see his family. As he walked, he noticed his heart was beating faster and faster. He was anxious. He imagined what it would be like at home after all this time. When he was in prison, his family would visit him every other month. He was excited to see them again without any restrictions, but it was stressful. It had been a long time since he'd last seen his house, his yard, his old room. He approached it now with gladness and some apprehension. He took a deep breath, steadied himself, and knocked on the door.

Time seemed to stand still. He could feel his heartbeat pulsing in his throat. He could hear it thudding in the space of silence between his knock and the nervous uncertainty of waiting for someone to answer. He was sweating as he heard footsteps approaching the front door. He took another deep breath.

"Who is it?" asked a woman's voice from behind the door.

"It's me. It's Mike," he responded. The door slowly opened. It was his mom. She greeted him with a huge smile and an even bigger hug.

"Oh my gosh! Mike!" she cried out, with tears in her eyes. "You have gotten so big. I can't believe my son is back in my life!" She looked at his face, taking in every detail. He was right there in front of her, a free man. "It's so good to hear your voice in person and not over the phone. Do you need anything? Are you hungry? Sit down, I'll make you a celebratory feast!"

Mike was extremely happy to see her so excited. He felt at peace in her presence, like he could finally exhale, and her cooking only enhanced that. She made a variety of Korean dishes for him: a beautiful array of colors, tastes, textures that all took him powerfully back to his childhood. It was too much food for one person, but Mike was up for the challenge. He was grateful for the food, for his home, for his mom. He was grateful that he didn't have to rush to eat or look over his shoulder. He could go back for seconds, thirds, or maybe even fourths, and he could eat until he was completely stuffed. Mike was finally home. The meal and the familiarity it brought with him helped a lot. The unease of earlier had left him as he settled into normalcy.

"I know you heard about what happened to your sister's boyfriend," his mother said. "I'm glad that you went to the shelter."

"Thank you," Mike replied. "I definitely felt like it was the best thing to do, to not be involved. What was the situation? Why did he get shot?" It was then that he really noticed how quiet the house was and that he hadn't seen his sister. "Where's Amy now? Is she ok?" Mike asked.

"Amy's fine, she's at the hospital with him," she replied. She narrowed her eyes and shot him a warning glance. "You don't need to worry about that situation. It's none of your business."

"I hear you loud and clear," Mike responded, chuckling to himself. "As long as Amy is fine, I'm good. Plus, I'm not looking to get into any trouble."

"I know you're not," she replied, her face softening. "That's why you're staying indoors until we figure out a plan for you."

Mike smiled and said: "I have a plan. I'll get a job and work my way up. I already filled out a few applications."

"Oh, really?" she replied, with a surprised look on her face "Well, you're two steps ahead of me," she laughed. "I was going to allow you to get used to the world again before pushing you out to work. When did this change come about?"

Mike paused, a weary look on his face. "I'm just tired, Ma. I'm tired of living the way I did. I can't take it anymore. Prison isn't for me. I'm done."

She got up from the table and gave Mike another long, warm hug. She still couldn't believe that she was holding her son in her arms again.

There were times in prison where Mike felt like his actions were going to cause him to get more time, but he was able to fight through it. Life looked promising: no more bland foods, no more waking up when he didn't want to, no more sharing living space with strangers, no more prison. Mike felt as if God was giving him a second chance and it was up to him to stay on the right path. Mom didn't want to let go of him.

His mom got a phone call. "Tomorrow is the Fourth of July?" she was asking. "I could have sworn today was the second." She pulled out a small green notebook, saying: "let me check my calendar. Guess what? Mike is finally home! He looks so healthy! He'll definitely be coming tomorrow. We can't wait to see you guys! Ok, see you tomorrow." She turned back to Mike: "Your aunt is throwing a barbecue for the Fourth of July, and she would love to see you. I'm sure everyone else would love to see you, too, so you're going," she said joyfully. "Go to your room. See if any of your clothes still fit. Everything should be exactly how you left it, just a little cleaner."

In his room, Mike was overwhelmed by nostalgia. The first thing he did was sit on his bed. It was so soft and comfortable. He had a thick mattress, beautiful bedding, plush pillows.

Now this is exactly what a bed should feel like, he thought to himself.

Before he knew it, he fell into a deep sleep. All the excitement and nervousness had tired him out. He went to sleep in his shoes. For the first time in a long while he was able to get a proper night's rest. He woke up around midnight to the sound of firecrackers marking the exact moment that July 3rd became July 4th. This began the celebration for the day. Locals in his neighborhood always bought fireworks for entertainment. Mike watched until the fireworks quieted down and as the neighbors' revelries died out, he went back to his comfortable, warm bed. Under the covers, his mind eased, and he fell back to sleep with no problem.

III

The sun was out, the birds were chirping, and the comforting smell of breakfast was drifting through the house.

"Mike, wake up, we have to go soon," Mom yelled as she shook him awake. He didn't like that at all. It reminded him of prison. Getting woken up was like hell to him. His mom could see how much he disliked it and allowed him to sleep as long as he wanted.

"Whenever you're ready, Mike. Breakfast is waiting for you," she said. "Your sister is home, too. She's doing fine, and all is well with her boyfriend. He's expected to make a full recovery."

It was impossible for Mike to go back to sleep now, but he still didn't move. He just lay there, enjoying the freedom of not having to get up. He closed his eyes for a minute, thinking about how grateful he was. 45 minutes flew by before his mom called him again. He was finally ready to get up. He brushed his teeth and went straight to the dining room. After his breakfast, he got ready for the barbecue. Another necessity that Mike greatly appreciated was showering for however long he wanted, whenever he wanted. He was also immensely grateful to have hot water.

He stepped out of the shower and rifled through his closet looking for something to wear. He hoped to find something that fit, but most of his clothes were too small. He settled on a tracksuit that he had bought years ago but had never worn because it was too big. He was glad he had kept it because now it fit him perfectly. He had worked out a lot in prison. When he came home everyone was impressed with his physique.

Mike went into the kitchen to help pack food and condiments for the barbecue. He was anxious and excited to see his family. He was unsure about how to act in a social setting since it had been so long. The ride to the barbecue was quiet, but the vibe was relaxed and easy. He wondered which job was going to call him back. He thought about the food at the barbecue. He wondered who would be there. He thought about all the things he wanted to do now that he was out.

When they arrived, everyone turned to look at them. He could feel his pulse in his throat. Social anxiety was creeping up on him. This was his first large social gathering since prison. He had to remind himself that this was his family, not other inmates. He took a deep breath, doing his best to adapt. He had missed them so much and they missed him. He felt like all the attention was on him. He felt completely out of his element. He felt that prison mentality creeping into his thoughts, and he had to consciously turn it away, constantly reminding himself he was among family and friends and that he was safe and loved here.

"Mike!" his aunt yelled from across the yard. "My baby!" she exclaimed. "It's been so long. We've missed you so much. Your mom was right, you have been taking really good care of yourself."

"Thank you," was all Mike could say. He wanted to get out of his head and be like everyone else enjoying the sunshine, the food, the company. Instead, he felt anxious and awkward. In reality the vibes at the party were very relaxed and welcoming. He kept telling himself that he had no reason to be nervous. He told himself, *fuck it: I don't care what anyone thinks. I can only do my best.*

The whole family gathered around him as if he were a celebrity. He still felt out of place, but he also felt the family's reaction to seeing him was pure, genuine love. It was like everyone wanted to reconnect and catch up with him. Once everything settled down, Mike was able to find a quiet place to absorb and process everything. While eating, he thought about how supportive his family was. Seeing them warmed his heart, made him feel strong. It was just going to take time to reintegrate.

Mike's cousin, Angela, came over, happy to see him and excited for his new freedom.

"Hey, Mike, how's it going? How does it feel to be

out? Have you done anything fun yet?" she asked.

"No, I haven't had time, but hopefully soon," Mike replied.

"Well, a few friends and I are going to that waterpark, Splish Splash, next week. You should come and enjoy yourself," she said. "Here, take my number." Angela took Mike's phone and put her number in his contacts. She called herself from his phone to lock in his number. He was reluctant to accept the invitation, but didn't know how to say no. It seemed like less of an invitation and more of an obligation. Angela handed his phone back and said: "I'll hit you up. It was so good seeing you."

He nodded his head. "Same here, looking forward to it." Angela walked off to continue socializing and, a few moments later, Mike noticed an unfamiliar face. It was a woman he had never seen before. She couldn't have been family because he would've known her. She must have been a family friend. He wanted to go up to her and introduce himself, but he still didn't feel secure enough to speak to a woman. It had been years since he'd spoken to a woman. He really wanted to say something but couldn't think of anything. He needed time to warm up to a conversation with a complete stranger.

He watched the woman go up to Angela and hug her as if they were well-acquainted. The woman looked over and made eye contact with him for a few moments before she continued chatting. There was something special about that glance. It stirred up strong, strange feelings. He felt relieved that Angela knew who she was. That could be his way in. He didn't have the guts to talk to her. It was going to take time, eventually it would be easier.

She was beautiful. She had tan skin, big eyes and wavy hair, and a great personality and attitude. She did not look Asian to Mike. If anything, she looked like she could be mixed; maybe Spanish, like Puerto Rican or Dominican. Mike was immediately drawn to her. He sensed something different about her but did not know what. He was vexed. He knew he was staring but was helpless to stop. He was utterly transfixed by her beauty and felt a strong compulsion pushing him towards her. His nerves made him pause. He was caught in a panic by the mere sight of her and he had never experienced anything so powerful. Everything, every impulse in his mind was screaming at him to go forward and speak to her. His legs were dead, his mouth was dry, his breathing labored and rapid. He couldn't move. He had never felt fear like this, and it was exciting. He just knew he was staring at the woman who was about to become his wifey.

The barbecue ended without him saying a word to this mystery woman. He helped his mom clean up and put all the food away. They wrapped some leftovers to take back with them, said goodnight to everyone, got in the car and drove back home. In the passenger seat Mike leaned his head against the window, each passing streetlight flashing a streaky strobe across his face then quickly disappearing into darkness. He still felt a subtle electricity from the eye contact he made with his cousin's friend. He felt a rush thinking about the next time he would see her. Despite his apprehensions, he was still going to reach out to Angela to find out more about her intriguing friend.

They pulled up to the house. Mike was exhausted. It had been a long day and he had experienced a lot of stimulation. He took a shower, got in bed, and closed his eyes. At that moment, he was exactly where he wanted to be.

IV

The next morning, Mike was in the kitchen when he heard a knock at the door. He looked through the peephole and was surprised to see his old cellmate, Shorty Roc. Shorty had told Mike that he was going to come check up on him after he was released. Some people are all talk, so Mike didn't have any expectations. He couldn't believe that Shorty had shown up. This was one of the realest dudes he'd ever met.

Shorty Roc was from Queens, and he and Mike

built a tight bond while they did their time together. Shorty had been released a year before Mike, and each month he would send Mike $50 and some pictures to help ease his isolation.

"Shorty? How are you, man?" Mike said, in utter astonishment.

"Yo, Mike. What did I tell you?"

Mike and Shorty gave each other dap.

"I can't believe you're really here. How have you been?"

"I've been doing good, man. I'm doing good. Go get dressed and let's seize the day."

Shorty and Mike went to the beach, got lunch, went around Shorty's hood in Queens. Nothing big, but it was still an amazing day. To just be out and travelling around with Shorty was pure joy. Mike took in the summer sun, felt it healing him, its beams friendly and familiar upon his smiling face.

Shorty was showing Mike off to every friend in the neighborhood. Shorty had already bigged Mike up and co-signed him to his peers, so they accepted him.

"Mike is the realest Asian motherfucker I know," Shorty professed.

The kids from Queens already knew about Mike because of the stories Shorty Roc had told them. It was great for Mike to spend time with an old friend; someone positive who was doing well for himself. He felt totally comfortable around Shorty. Now that they were both free men, they were getting to enjoy life, and things felt right again.

Shorty and Mike went to Far Rockaway Beach. They talked about their time upstate and what the future held for them. Shorty offered Mike some weed but Mike declined.

"I just came home. I'm not trying to jeopardize my freedom."

Shorty said: "True, my bad. What are your plans, Mike?"

"One step at a time."

V

A day had passed since the Fourth of July barbecue, and the mystery woman was still on Mike's mind. He decided to text Angela to see if she could tell him a little more about her and possibly link the two of them together. He texted his cousin, asking if she knew the woman.

Angela's response came back swiftly: *"That was my close friend, her name is Honey. I saw you guys make eye contact a couple of times. She had an eye for you! She's going to be coming to Splish Splash with us! Here, take her number, I'll let her know that I gave her yours and that you'll text her."*

Mike was nervous about texting Honey. He didn't want to seem desperate, so he decided to wait two days. In the meantime, he distracted himself by waiting on callbacks from potential jobs. He felt less confident and more sluggish from being in the house all the time. Freedom wasn't feeling as good as he thought it would. The transformation from the excitement of being free to the everyday grind of routine was hitting him hard and sitting on his shoulders like a weight. Trying to get a job hadn't been as easy as he had hoped. He regretted disclosing that he had been convicted of a felony. He felt almost certain that this was the reason no one had called him back yet. Another day went by, and he finally decided to text Honey. He steeled himself for the action and braced for rejection, or worse: indifference.

Hey Honey, this is Mike, Angela's cousin. We saw each other at the barbecue, his initial text began.

Hey, Mike! I've been waiting for your text. How are you? she responded. It came almost instantly, which Mike took as a good omen.

For the next few days, they continued to text and to tentatively get to know each other. Mike was extremely cautious with his questions and answers. He didn't want to give too much of himself away. The waterpark trip was just around the corner, and they were both excited. They continued texting, and through their digital conversations they grew closer. This was all new for Mike, and he was nervous. He was also excited.

On the day of the trip Mike wore his brand new, all-white Uptowns and a fresh outfit. He felt good. Confident. While they waited in line, the manager glanced down at Mike's Uptowns and told him he couldn't come into the park unless he wore swimming shoes or sandals. Feeling inconvenienced and slightly embarrassed, he and Angela drove to a nearby mall to find some swim shoes. He found the perfect pair and they headed back.

Honey was there waiting and, again, Mike was struck by her beauty. It literally sucked the breath from his lungs, and he had to inhale deeply to steady his nerves. On the outside, though, he was cool. Honey greeted Mike and Angela with a big smile.

"You guys took forever," she said.

"It's all Mike's fault, we had to drive to the mall to get him swimming shoes," Angela explained, teasingly.

"No worries," Honey laughed. "Let's just get in the water, this sun is killing me."

They got their tickets and put their stuff in some lockers. Mike took his shirt off. When he turned around, he saw Honey in her bathing suit, and it shocked him. It had been years since he'd seen so much exposed skin on a woman. He was stunned by how beautiful she was. Just like that, his anxiety was gone. He felt a sense of calm wash over him. He wanted to tell her how beautiful she was right then and there but didn't want her to feel creeped out. Honey turned around and saw Mike staring at her, but he was too deep in his daydream to notice.

"You look great, Mike. Do you work out?" Honey asked, giving him a flirty look.

"Yes, I do. Almost every day for three years straight," said Mike. He felt more confident around her. He was engaged in conversation and making full eye contact. It terrified him, but he was doing it. He couldn't think of a single thing that was happening outside of just being there with Honey. Everything around them seemed to stand still and then melt away. He found her boldness, her easy familiarity towards him very exciting. As they stood in line for a water slide, Honey looked up at Mike.

"I'm so nervous," Honey said with a playful laugh.

"Don't be nervous, I'm here with you. I got you," Mike said, grabbing her hand. To his surprise, she didn't let go. The ease with which he moved excited her. Her acceptance thrilled him. There was an instant connection as soon as their hands touched. It was undeniable. Persistent.

"It definitely looks like it's going to be fun, though. Are you excited?" She looked him directly in his eyes.

"Definitely," said Mike. Although the slide looked

cool, all the excitement he was feeling was from being with Honey.

"I really want to get to know you more, will I see you after today?" Honey asked.

"Yes, of course. Let's go see a movie. When are you free?"

"The weekends, usually," she said.

"Ok, cool, let's do it this weekend," Mike said with a smile.

"Cool, it's a date. I wanted to ask, have you found a job yet? Angela told me about your situation, and I'd like to help," she offered.

Mike replied: "No, not yet. I've filled out a few applications. I'm still waiting on some calls."

"Cool, no worries, we'll get you a job," Honey said. They spent the entire day together and learned more about each other. That was what Mike found most exciting: learning all the little, inconsequential things about her. By the time they left, they both knew what they had together was special.

VI

As time went by, Mike and Honey went on more dates and spent more and more time together. They opened up to each other and Mike was able to confide in her about his past and how he viewed life. He spoke to her about his decision to become a better person. His openness inspired her and made her want to be a part of his life. Honey became more interested in Mike the deeper they talked. For Mike, the talking helped draw him out, to make him feel normal, like he belonged. With Honey he felt like he had a place in this world.

She kept her word about helping him get a job. She knew about practical things: she suggested some new clothes for interviews. She took him shopping and drove him around to all his interviews. After weeks of searching, he was finally able to land a position as a dishwasher at an Outback Steakhouse. It wasn't an ideal job, but Mike was still thankful that he was able to make his own money in a legal way. As a dishwasher, he was making $11 an hour. It was pocket change to him, but he hoped to get a raise by putting in the time and effort.

A few months went by, and he was able to save enough for a car. With a car came even more responsibility. He would have to pay for gas, insurance, and all the expenses required to keep a car on the road. He wouldn't be able to make the payments on time since he was making so little.

Eventually, an opportunity came for him to work on the grill permanently. Outback's grillers made $20 an hour. Mike found that out from the previous guy who was on the grill. When his manager presented him with the opportunity, Mike accepted the new job right away. He was expecting a large pay increase. When he got his paycheck, he was shocked to see that he was still being paid the same rate as a dishwasher. He was confused and slightly angry. He immediately confronted his manager.

"I just wanted to touch base with you because I think there's been a mistake on my check," said Mike.

"Mistake?" replied his manager.

"Yes, a mistake. On my check. I worked the grill this whole week, expecting a pay increase, and my check says my pay is still $11 an hour. It should be $20 an hour."

"How about you just be a team player, Mike? It's not all about the money," he replied with a smirk That last remark, coupled with his infuriating, smug smirk, ignited Mike's ire and caused the two of them to argue. Mike felt his blood boiling. He felt anger throughout his body. He was facing a choice: quit on the spot or continue to be taken advantage of by his asshole boss.

He quit.

"I don't need this disrespect. You're fucking taking advantage of me. I quit!" Mike was screaming now, and he didn't care who heard him.

"Quit and go where?" the manager asked derisively, mocking Mike and his record. "Nobody wants a criminal working for them. You're lucky I even allowed you in here!" He was now screaming, too. Mike felt the heat at the back of his brain – the signal that the rage was about to take over in a vicious blackout. His conscious mind was receding into brilliant white light as the violence bubbled on the top of his brain like warm ginger ale. Slowly his fists balled into rock-hard sledgehammers. He knew what was coming. And then…

He took a deep, deep breath.

A deep, deep pause.

His eyes opened. He exhaled. It was gone. A serene, knowing calm replaced the rage. A clarity replaced the muddled thoughts of violence. His heartbeat slowed to a crawl. Everything slowed down and he let it go. He let the anger go and turned his back. He walked.

Mike didn't say a word. He went straight home. When he went back to Outback, he kept his anger buried. He had quelled the immediate rage the night before, but the anger had settled deep in the pit of his stomach. From there it added on some passing travelers – anxiety, regret, shame… the usual shit. He tried to distract himself by just concentrating on the work. He went back as a dishwasher for a few more weeks. He was stuck in the hierarchy that most kitchens employ: once you are in the back of the house you do what's needed, regardless of station or job description. Mike had had experience working in the kitchen upstate, so they eventually moved him to the food line. That didn't work out either and Mike quit for good.

Amy's boyfriend, Jay, had recovered from the worst of his injuries after the shooting and had gone back to his job delivering milk. He drove his milk truck to the local stores and supermarkets. Lifting and carrying the heavy cases of milk was proving to be too much for him due to his still-healing injuries. Jay would drive the truck and Mike would do the heavy lifting. The job only paid a little bit more than dishwashing, and Mike wasn't really motivated. He quit after a short while. He was going to pursue a real estate license.

Mike wanted to start buying and flipping houses. He knew he could make at least $20,000 a house. It was something he had read about, and it seemed like a natural choice for him. He spoke to friends who had experience flipping houses. These were cats that knew him well, and every one of them thought Mike could be successful in that game. They directed him on how to get started, who to know, how to act, what to look for and when to be cautious. In a lot of ways his education was similar to the influence and the schooling he had received running the streets as a kid. It was all basically the same game.

In his first month, Mike was able to flip one house. This really motivated him. New agents had to wait two months to receive the money from a sale, and Mike needed his money to come quickly. He had to decide, either try his best, live clean, wait it out and be broke (but stress-free), or risk everything and return to his old ways. He was a free man now. He was with his family and friends again, his relationship with Honey was going great. He was seeing how much he had to lose by going back into the streets. For the first time in his life, Mike was starting to look at the bigger picture.

VII

Mike found himself faced with a difficult, risky, and potentially life-changing decision. He had decided to sell weed on the side.

This was a big decision for Mike. He knew what he was risking. He had a plan to keep it small and contained within a tight circle of friends. No outsiders. He only sold to people he knew from his neighborhood. This was not a venture he was trying to extend for a long period of time. He just needed to get on his feet. His lack of funds was hindering him in so many aspects. He hated having to ask Honey for rides. He hated that his time was never his own. He had earned his freedom from prison but being broke was its own kind of prison. Sometimes it was just as demoralizing. That legit money is a slow grind, especially for someone like him.

When Honey had to pay for some of their dates, it really got to him. He felt small. He felt like a loser. He was not the kind of man to let a woman pay for a date and it did not sit well with him. His self-esteem had been taking some big hits ever since he got out. It was like one kick to the gut after another. He knew one of the most basic keys to his success was building this relationship with Honey. He instinctually knew how crucial it was to his survival. With Honey he felt he had a chance at redemption. He knew himself so much better after talks with her. He liked himself when he was with her. He never had to pretend. Before, his entire life had been about dishonesty, both intellectual and emotional. Before, his feelings were non-existent because life made it that way; *his* life had made it that way by demanding a strict regimen of calloused, emotionless distance, even from the people he loved.

In prison Mike learned how to keep that outer shell indurated and impenetrable out of necessity. It had been the same when he was in the streets. He had a lot of psychological hardness that he needed to deal with before he could become the kind of man that deserved to be with someone like Honey. And, before he could even begin to deal with any of it, he had to get his feet on level ground. He needed money for the basic human necessities of life and if that meant doing something drastic and risky, so be it. If it was for Honey, then it was the right thing to do.

Mike knew what he was risking, but he made the choice to sell weed anyway. He rationalized it, he brushed aside all thoughts of getting caught or going back and focused on the future.

VIII

Six months went by, and Mike was still selling bud. The extra money was really helping him. But he was on parole, and if he got caught, he'd end up right back in prison. He kept telling himself that he would stop soon but it was helping so much.

The day finally came that Mike decided to stop. He was now making enough money legitimately that he could leave the weed business behind and concentrate on real estate. He had been building up a nice chunk of savings and he was starting to feel good about moving forward.

Not long after his decision to retire, he got a text from a customer named Jon. Jon was a janitor and he had been buying large quantities of weed from Mike over the past few months. It crossed Mike's mind that there was something suspicious about Jon. Something that he couldn't put his finger on, but he didn't see him as a threat. But, this time, Jon had texted with an unusual request.

Can you get me white?

Mike knew what that meant, and he knew all the hassles that came along with such a request. He didn't even want to entertain the thought.

Nah, I don't fuck with that, Mike responded.

Can you just do me one favor then? I want to get more bud from you, but on your way can you pick up some white from my guy and bring it with you? It's totally cool and I'll totally make it worth your while $$$$.

I can bring the weed to you, but not the white.

Please? My guy will bring it to you, and you can bring it to me. I'm going to have a friend meet you real quick. He's gonna give you the money, you give him everything and he will give it to me. I'm seriously gonna hook you up for doing this for me.

Mike hesitated. He knew it was dangerous. Fucking with that white girl put you in a whole other class of felony. He also knew cokeheads were sketchy and unpredictable and a real fucking pain in the balls to deal with. He didn't need the stress. But he did need the money, and his eyes kept going back to the dollar signs in Jon's text.

Fuck it.

Aiight, no doubt. Just this one time, though.

It was cast, and whatever was going to come was going to come. Jon was a big customer. He had put a lot of money in Mike's pocket, and Mike wanted to keep him happy. He agreed to meet the friend with the coke. Mike briefly considered bringing along a weapon because coke dealers were notoriously shady and paranoid, especially if they were users. Since their meeting was in public, Mike decided it wouldn't be necessary. The meet went down without incident. The guy was strictly business, just the way Mike liked.

Mike had the product and was waiting in his car. He was cautious, but not nervous. He figured the difficult part was already over. All he had to do was collect his money and get the fuck out of there.

He was there for less than a minute before he heard: "Put your hands up and step out of the car! Move slowly!"

And there it was.

His mind raced. He wondered if Jon was an informant. He *knew* Jon was an informant.

Mike hung his head as the cops first searched him and then his car. They tore his shit apart, taking particular glee in wrecking the interior of the car. Once they found what they were looking for, they cuffed him and threw him in the back of the car.

Once again, Mike was back in police custody.

Chapter 2: New York State of Mind

I

How could he put himself in this situation again? His life was finally going well. He had a legal job in real estate He had been staying away from trouble, making all his PO appointments, staying sober, and he had a girlfriend that he loved. Why was he taking such stupid risks when he was getting steadily closer to being a free man?

He didn't know how to tell Honey he was selling again. He knew it would break her heart and, worse, would make her leave him. He was sure of that. He thought about how badly he was disappointing the people he loved, the people who had stood up for him and stood by him and had taken care of him while he was away. He also let himself down.

Mike wondered if anyone besides Jon had snitched on him. His mind raced thinking about all the people he had served the last couple of days. Nobody seemed suspicious except Jon. It *had* to be Jon. Mike was already planning revenge, and his plan was particularly violent. As the police car drove on, Mike realized that it was taking an unusual route to the station.

"Where are we going?" he asked.

"Shut the fuck up," one of the officers yelled at him.

"We just passed the turn that goes to the police station. Where are you taking me?" Mike asked.

The officer coldly replied: "You're going straight downtown to the District Attorney's office. You got caught. Possession of a class B substance. Things aren't looking good for you."

Mike was nervous. He knew he was going to be detained at Rikers Island. The police were talking to Mike the whole way downtown, but he stayed silent. They peppered him with questions trying to trick him into admitting something. He knew the deal. It was like scripted dialogue from a bad film. Mike almost laughed at them, but he didn't want to make things worse. His demeaner remained stoic, stolid, and impenetrable. His mind slowed to a precise, deliberate, and analytic speed. He coolly assessed his situation with no panic whatsoever. Panic makes you talk. Panic makes you commit to stupid decisions. These were not conscious thoughts in Mike's head, rather an entire skill set of instinct had kicked in and taken over every part of his mind and body. They drove on, the cops taunting and threatening him the entire time.

Upon arrival, they threw him into an interrogation room and started questioning him, asking:

"Where did you get the coke? Why were you at that

location? Who gave it to you?" He knew that this was part of a much bigger bust. He knew his rights and remained silent.

"Look, Mike: if you snitch, we will let you off easy."

Mike only said: "I want to speak to my lawyer."

"Just fucking speak, God damn it!" one of the officers screamed. "Tell me or you are going to jail!" Bad cop was pounding his fist on the table dramatically, his face so close to Mike's that Mike could smell his coffee breath and cheap body spray.

Mike stayed silent.

"You don't want to speak?" the officer continued. "Okay, cool. We'll give you a deal. How much money do you want?" They were still trying to play good cop/bad cop and Mike was still not willing to cooperate. He stared blankly into the officer's face and, in a low, assured voice, repeated:

"I want to speak to my lawyer. This is not my first time, pig."

"Oh, you a gangsta'?" The cop retorted. "The deal's off."

"What deal?" Mike asked sarcastically.

"Take him out of here."

Mike and a few other men were being packed into a police van headed to Rikers Island. He was already mentally preparing himself. He knew what to do. He would keep a low profile in jail and not start trouble with anyone. He'd probably be in for two or three days. He would post bail and they would give him more parole time. In Rikers they put him in OBCC (Otis Bantum Correctional Center). Inmates took over the acrostic and restructured it to mean "Only Bloods Can Control." The house that Mike was placed in was called 8 Mile. 8 Mile was run by gang members affiliated with the Bloods. Mike was the only Asian in the house.

He wanted to use the phone so he could call Honey or his sister. The house he was placed in had three phones. The first phone was a neutral phone, which people who weren't gang-affiliated used. The second phone was a Spanish phone, which was run by the Latin Kings. The third phone was used exclusively by the Bloods. Mike didn't want any problems, so he waited for the neutral phone. After waiting for an hour, there was still a long line of people ahead of him. He knew he wouldn't be able to use the phone until tomorrow. He felt frustrated and desperate. The line for the Spanish phone was short, and the line for the Bloods' phone was completely empty. There was no one in sight, so he decided to use the Bloods' phone. Mike had been locked up before and knew if he used that phone, it would be a problem. He was determined to make the call.

As soon as he walked over to use the phone he was

immediately confronted.

"Yo, who you? This is the Bloods' phone. You can't use this."

Mike made eye contact with him and replied: "No disrespect, I understand how jail rules go, but I really need to call my lawyer and my family."

"Where are you from?" the inmate asked.

"Brooklyn," Mike replied.

"Okay, cool, make it quick. I'll give you a few minutes," said the inmate.

Mike was grateful for this kind gesture and quickly called Amy. He explained the situation and told her he had court in three days. He was sure he'd be bailed out easily. He called Honey and told her what happened. Honey was pissed off and disappointed.

"How could you get yourself into trouble like this again? You had a job. Why would you go back to this kind of stuff, Mike?" Although she was furious with him, she wanted to help him. After a short pause she said, softly: "How much is your bail?"

"I don't know yet. I have court in three days. I should be good, though. Bail will most likely be a few thousand," he answered. "I'll call you back in a few days and let you know what's going on with everything. Just stay close to your phone. I'll try to call you around the same time every day, so you know it's me."

"I love you, Mike. Please stay out of trouble in there."

"I love you, Honey."

Mike hung up with Honey and was about to call his lawyer, when an inmate from the Blood side of the house screamed: "Yo, who's this Asian dude on the phone?"

Mike said nothing and put the phone on the hook. With a resigned sigh he turned around and went to his cell to pack his belongings because he thought it was about to get popping. He knew fighting in jail would mean more time. He wasn't scared at all, but he didn't want any more problems. As expected, a few Blood inmates followed Mike to his cell.

"Yo, who told you that you could use that phone?" one of the Blood inmates asked.

"One of your homies said it was cool," said Mike.

"Nah, fuck that. It's not cool with us."

An uproar broke out in the cell block, and everyone crowded around to see what was happening. They could smell the conflict in the air, and it drew them out. It was an unspoken, collective imperative, and just about every inmate responded.

Mike and the Bloods were going back and forth, leading more Bloods to rush over. Mike knew that he had made a bad decision and now he had to face the consequences.

"Yo, wassup, Mike?" Someone called to him from the crowd of Bloods. "He's good here. Nobody touch him." The voice had the rough edge of authority.

Mike was still confused as to who was calling his name. The man came closer. Mike realized it was a friend from his neighborhood. The man, whose name was Mel, had grown up in the same hood as Mike. Mel knew that even though Mike was Asian he put in work in the streets. He knew Mike's reputation and they had some people in common. Once the Bloods realized that Mel and Mike were cool, they began to calm down and listen to Mel. Mel explained that Mike was affiliated with him, and the other Bloods dispersed. Mike and Mel greeted each other.

"Yo, Mike, how you ended up here?"

"I got caught up in a drug charge. What about you?"

"Caught with a dirty pistol," Mel said. "I'm sorry for the little altercation, it won't happen again. I'm second in command in the house and anything I say goes. You need anything?"

"Yeah, I need to call my lawyer," Mike said.

"Aiight cool, you do that." He turned towards the crowd and issued a proclamation: "Yo, I got an announcement. Y'all see this Asian dude? He with *me*. Anybody got a problem you can come handle it with me." Mel was screaming, making sure every last inmate in the entire cell block heard him and heard him well.

Over the next few days, Mike and Mel became more acquainted. Mel spoke about getting out soon. He introduced Mike to other Blood inmates. Mike gained respect in jail through Mel telling stories about him. Mel gave them the rundown of the important stuff: How active Mike was in the streets, the respect he had in the hood, and how, even though he was Asian, he fucked with Black and Spanish girls. The other Bloods were surprised by Mike. They had never met a hood Asian like him before.

There were set days for visitations on Rikers Island. Visitation privileges were determined by the first initial of your last name. Mike saw that he was up for a visit on Friday, so he asked Honey if she would come up.

Honey came up to Rikers with Mike's sister. Amy had been to Rikers before, so she knew her way around. The moment he saw Honey and Amy, he apologized profusely, telling them how disappointed he was in himself. Honey couldn't even look at him.

"This just doesn't seem real," she said.

"It's damn real. I'm never coming back here again. You will never have to come see me in jail ever again," Mike reassured her. Looking at Honey's face he could tell she was uncomfortable. Mike knew he fucked up big time.

The second time she visited Mike, Honey came by herself. Amy couldn't come because she was working. Honey was a little more comfortable this time. She and

Mike spent the visit just holding hands and talking about their future together.

Soon it was time for Mike's court appearance. They set his bail at $100,000. Mike didn't have that kind of money. Luckily, he had a great lawyer, and he was able to get a bail reduction. At first, his lawyer asked for 75% percent bail reduction. The judge denied the request and was willing to give a 50% reduction. They still thought it was too high for the charge. The judge was eventually willing to meet in the middle with a 65% reduction. Mike would have to pay $35,000 for bail, plus lawyer fees. He had to pay that in full because he was ineligible for a bond due to his previous bid. The set bail was still remarkably high, but he figured that he could make a few calls and get the money. As soon as he got back from court, he looked for Mel. He asked a few of the inmates if they'd seen him, and a few said he got paroled. Mike was happy for him.

Mike went straight for the phone. He figured since he had become cordial with the some of the Bloods, he would still be able to use their phone. As soon as he picked up the phone a young voice yelled: "Yo, Mel ain't here no more. Get off our phone or it's going to be a problem." Mike looked over and saw that the threats were coming from a dude who looked like he lived to start trouble.

Mike replied: "A problem with who? I've been using this phone for the last couple of days, and I've had no problems." The young Blood got up and stepped to Mike, getting right up in his face. He told Mike that if he didn't hang up the phone the situation was going to get violent. Once the other Bloods heard this, they got up and came over, trying to diffuse the situation and let Mike use the phone.

"He's good. We know he knows Mel. Let him slide," said one of the Blood inmates. The young Blood was still screaming: "If we let him slide then we going to let the next person slide and I'm not letting that fucking happen."

"Shut the fuck up," Mike screamed back at him.

The situation escalated as they became more heated. Mike stepped to the young Blood's face ready to fight. The other Bloods got up and stepped between them.

"No, don't break it up," Mike was yelling. "If he wants to fight then let's fight."

"Nah, we can't let that happen," one of the Bloods responded. "If one Blood fights, we all fight. That's jail house rules. You either allow us to defuse the situation, or we gonna' have to do what has to be done."

Mike knew the deal. He was hot, but he knew what the outcome would be if he fought the young Blood. It was not in his nature to walk away or to back down, but he had no choice. It made his stomach churn and his anger rise.

"I understand," said Mike through gritted teeth. He turned back to the phone and started dialing.

The Bloods, still in a tizzy, continued arguing among themselves while attempting to calm the young Blood down. After all that, the young Blood finally decided to let Mike use the phone out of respect for Mel.

Mike called his family and close friends for help, explaining his situation and how much his bail was. He promised everyone he would pay them back. Mike was known for getting money, so no one hesitated to give him cash. In one day, he was able to get enough to make bail. He received most of the money from his immediate family, his close friend Shorty Roc, and his girl. Once all the money cleared and was transferred, Mike was released the next day around 2 a.m. he was greeted by Amy, Honey, and Shorty Roc. Honey looked distraught. She greeted him with a long hug, grabbing him as tightly as she possibly could, her eyes filled with tears.

"I missed you so much, are you okay, babe?"

"Yeah, I'm just happy to be out," he replied. "Being in jail was just another reminder of how much freedom means to me."

"Mike, are you hungry?" asked Shorty Roc.

"I don't have too much of an appetite."

Shorty gave him $100 to get food and maintain himself for the next couple of days. Mike was grateful to be surrounded by such wonderful, supportive people and unconditional love.

Amy looked exhausted and barely said a word. She yawned multiple times during the car ride and couldn't wait to get home. Mike convinced Honey to come to his place for the night. There was no mention of Mike selling again. Honey just seemed happy to be with him. They spoke about being together and how she didn't want him going back to the streets. She told him that she refused to continue dealing with him if he was going to be in and out of jail. He promised it wouldn't happen again.

Mike knew his parole officer would be pissed and would be on his back more than ever on his next visit. He was mostly worried about paying back all the money he owed. The real estate game seemed promising, and was great money, but it just wasn't coming fast enough for him. For the next two days, Mike decided to lay low and spend time with Honey. He didn't leave his house at all. They just chilled, watched movies, and enjoyed each other.

On Monday morning, Mike woke up to his phone being blown up by his parole officer. Feeling uneasy, he called her back, and prepared himself for the worst.

"Hello, Ms. Hubbert." His voice was barely a whisper.

"Hello, Mike. I heard about everything that happened and we need to touch base and talk about this," said Ms. Hubbert. "Can you come into the office around noon?"

"Today is Halloween, so I won't be here at all,"

Mike replied.

"Come now if you can, it's urgent," she pleaded.

"I'll be there soon."

Mike wondered if she understood his predicament. The best situation right now was to get more parole time until his next court appearance. Having to check in with Ms. Hubbert at least twice a week and being subjected to random drug tests was punishment enough.

While getting dressed, Amy called and asked if he could take her daughter, Cassy, trick or treating. Mike agreed but told her that it would have to be after he met his parole officer. Amy decided to go with Mike. She brought Cassy with her.

Mike was in the waiting area with his sister and Cassy. The secretary looked confused and awkward when she buzzed the door to let him in. He was greeted by Mrs. Hubbert. Her voice was extra chirpy. Something wasn't right. She wasn't asking questions like she usually did. She wouldn't make eye contact. They rode the elevator in awkward silence. As soon as the elevator doors opened there was a gang of police officers waiting. Mike was immediately detained and brought back downstairs.

Amy started screaming: 'Wait, what is happening?"

"He's going to jail," one of the police officers replied. He pushed his knee into Mike's back, handcuffing him.

"He's already been through the system. He just posted bailed two days ago, this is illegal," screamed Amy.

"Well, we're just following orders, ma'am. His parole officer thinks this is best for him." With his face planted on the cold floor, it finally dawned on Mike that the reason Ms. Hubbert pressed him to come to her office was to have him locked up. Mike was confused as to how he could be detained if he had already gone to jail and had been bailed out.

"You're locking me up for nothing, let me go." Mike's voice was muffled and angry.

"Parole violation," one of the officers said. "You came in contact with police, I'm pretty sure you know that's a violation of parole."

Mike was speechless. He didn't know what to think or do. At that moment, he had to let go of all control. He accepted his fate and was sent back to Rikers Island. He was put in the C74 building. C74 was called "Adolescents at War." It was called that because the YGs got busy. He was relieved that he didn't have to return to OBCC where he felt like bad blood was bound to stir back up.

Mike arrived at Rikers Island wearing a $300 Coogi sweater, $250 Evisu Jeans, and a fresh pair of Timbs. He was dressed for a party. It was different than the first time he was locked up. He hadn't looked as flashy then. Once again, Mike being Asian surprised a lot of the inmates.

He didn't feel anything threatening or worrisome. There were mostly dudes from Brooklyn, which made Mike even more comfortable. He looked around and saw a familiar face. The man's name was Moe, and he was from Crown Heights. The situation here was similar to the one in OBCC, except instead of Mel and the Bloods, Moe and his crew of people ran this house. Anything Mike wanted or needed to do; Moe was able to push the buttons for him. He had correction officers bringing cigarettes, Kentucky Fried Chicken, McDonald's. This house was a money house, and Moe and his friends were ballers. There were drugs, food, cigarettes, gambling… a lot of shit was going on in this house.

One of Moe's soldiers, Young Gunner, who was a Crip, couldn't believe that Mike was this hood-ass Asian dude.

"Damn, I've been locked up too long. Asian dudes is rocking Coogi and Evisu."

Mike and Moe burst out laughing. "This dude right here ain't Asian, he's Black, and I've seen him get busy. He's official," Moe said nodding at Mike. Young Gunner wanted to go to the yard to get some fresh air and work out. Mike also wanted to go outside. So, when the C.O. called "yard!" Young Gunner and Mike hit the pullup bar and the weights. On the way out there were two other houses sharing the yard with Mike's house. Young Gunner said:

"Mike, watch my back there's mad Bloods in the yard. "

At about 6 foot and 230 pounds, Mike was a big Asian guy. He had worked out constantly during his entire bid, so he still had size. Young Gunner was also pretty big, about 6 foot and 210 pounds, all ripped up. The Bloods knew he was a Crip, but they never tried anything because Young Gunner's brother was a well-known drug dealer who ran with the Bloods from Crown Heights. They would look at him yell out: "Crab! Hardback!" trying to intimidate him. He wanted to attack them for mocking him. Mike told him to be easy. "That's what they want you to do. Don't do what they expect you to do, do the unexpected."

"You right," Young Gunner said. "You sound like a Asian Malcolm X." They laughed and went back to their workout.

Mike was in C74 for two weeks before he could get a parole hearing. At the hearing, Mike's lawyer fought hard to get him out of jail. He explained to the judge it was Mike's first time coming into police contact in 18 months, and that most repeat offenders ended up back in jail within a few weeks. The lawyer spoke highly of Mike's job as a realtor, highlighting how Mike was helping the company flip houses. He had never missed an appointment with Ms. Hubbert, and he had never failed a drug test. Finally, his lawyer was able to get his parole reinstated. He would be able to go home. The lawyer told him he strongly believed he could beat this case as long as he cooperated and stayed away from the police. He gave Mike some transcripts and told him to look at them when he got home. Names that were supposed to have been whited-out on the transcript weren't, and of course Jon's name was there, just as Mike expected. He still had revenge on his mind, but he didn't know why his lawyer would give him the transcripts.

Mike was furious. He went looking for Jon, and after a few hours spinning blocks, Mike found him at a local park. He jumped out the whip, yelling: "I know you fucking snitched on me," while walking menacingly toward him, the full brunt of his anger apparent in his hulking frame.

Jon turned around, his eyes popping out of his head in complete shock. He saw death walking towards him. He saw murder and death set its eyes on him and walk with a deliberate purpose straight towards him. He couldn't believe Mike was out of jail.

"S-Snitch?" Jon was stuttering with fear. "W-Why would I snitch on my friend? Mike, how are you? Where have you been?"

The two went back and forth, arguing about whether Jon had set up Mike up. Jon kept denying it until Mike pulled out the transcripts and shoved them in Jon's face.

"How did you get this?" Jon asked, confused and

nervous.

"Don't worry about that. I just need you to come to my lawyer's office and tell him that I never sold you anything," said Mike. "After we deal with my lawyer, you're going to tell the police the same thing." Mike focused all his rage, all his intent into staring down Jon. He knew this was serious and he was afraid. Mike used every intimidation tactic he'd ever learned. Jon was soft and square and crumbled instantly. Terrified of what Mike was going to do to him, Jon agreed. Mike grabbed him by the collar of his shirt like he was lifting a puppy by the scruff of its neck. Jon was babbling apologies the whole time Mike dragged him.

They went to the lawyer. The lawyer was angry at Mike. "Why would you bring him here," he asked incredulously.

"Well, I mean, you gave me these transcripts with his name on it, so I figured you wanted me to confront him," Mike said.

"You have to get him out of here, leave right now!

Jon left immediately, avoiding eye contact with everyone. Mike was completely confused. "I thought you wanted me to bring him here."

"No, I wanted you to fucking do him in!"

Mike was stunned. He didn't know what to do. He never anticipated this. His head spun. What the fuck was this lawyer trying to do? Bury him? Did he need Jon gone for other reasons and was just using Mike to carry it out? This was fucked and Mike couldn't see a way out. He couldn't trust anyone. He left the office, completely forgetting about Jon. He felt like he was back at square one. He needed a new lawyer, someone he could trust (well, as much as one could trust a lawyer), and he needed money.

II

Mike went back to real estate, but he had a different plan. Instead of working for someone, he would flip houses on his own. He had an amazing credit score, so he was able to buy houses with no money down. Banks were offering an unprecedented 100% financing rate. Mike knew this was the time people were buying homes with no money down. The first two months were hard for him, but once he got the hang of it, he began making the type of money that he had been waiting for. He bought his first house in Sunset Park for $600,000 but received $100,000 at closing. The seller agreed to $500,000, but Mike got an appraisal and was able to get the difference at closing.

He made $150,000 in the next 15 months, saving almost every penny he had. He went to parole every week.

He had a new lawyer, David, and he kept in touch regularly to give and get updates.

Mike was starting to worry that he might not be able to beat this case. His lawyer was asking him to compromise and take time, or even snitch. Meanwhile, the stress, the pressure, it was all getting to Mike. He found himself spending way too much money trying to make himself feel better. He had hit an emotional wall; a numbness accompanied his resignation. He couldn't seem to make that next step.

He started spending large amounts from his savings on clothes, partying, and other random, unnecessary things. He got in touch with his old friends and started hanging out with them more. He started hitting clubs. He was getting drunk every weekend and spending his money on bottles. Feeling completely reckless, with the impending threat of being locked up looming, he started moving carelessly. He got into fights at the clubs. In the streets, Mike had always prided himself on being disciplined. Now, he felt like he was slipping all the time. He felt completely lost and had no idea what to do. He felt like he didn't have anything to live for, except Honey. She had been holding him down, and he was grateful. She didn't know about his exploits yet, but it was just a matter of time until she caught on. She was too smart not to. Still, he kept up with his reckless lifestyle, pushing any and every boundary he could find. Mike walked around like a raw, exposed nerve just waiting to jump at anything. His rational mind knew he needed to stop if he wanted Honey to stay with him, but he couldn't stop himself. It was like he was outside his body watching himself making bad decisions that he was powerless to stop.

He wanted to keep Honey in his life at all costs, and he wanted her to be with him even if he was going to jail. He wanted to propose. He was going to propose to Honey.

Chapter 3: A Modest Proposal

I

Mike bought Honey a gorgeous ring. He left the jewelry store and went to where she worked. He laid back, waiting for her to come outside. She was visibly excited and happy to see him and jumped into the car. He was nervous, scared, but excited. Honey got in the car under the supposition that Mike was taking her out for lunch. As Mike drove, Honey was talking in a nonstop stream about the banality of her day. This one always leaves a mess in the breakroom, that one is always gossiping… Mike didn't hear a word of it, his mind was running rampant. He was trying to find the exact words to propose to Honey. She didn't even notice he wasn't listening and kept on telling stories about her co-workers at light speed.

He pulled up to a red light, turned to Honey and blurted it out: "Honey, will you marry me?" There was a stunned silence that, to Mike, lasted a thousand years. It felt like the song on the radio stopped. He had never felt fear like this.

In reality it was barely a moment. The shock wore off in seconds as Honey burst into tears and said: "Yes, yes I will!"

Mike finally remembered to breathe.

II

For the next few weeks, Mike spent all his time and attention on Honey. He took her out to eat, bought her gifts, and showered her with love and affection in every way possible. He stopped hanging out with his friends and put more time into the relationship. He re-dedicated himself to keeping straight and out of trouble. Honey was his strength, and now that she was to become his wife, he had an even stronger motivation to live right. He had two major paths to stick to – to build his life with his new wife and to beat his case in any way possible.

After a year and a half going back and forth to

court, things weren't looking good. On his last court date, they had told him they were ready for pre-trial. He was nervous now that the date was approaching. Despite the happiness and promise of a future with Honey, thoughts of going back to prison haunted him and a black despair born of helplessness settled in the pit of his stomach. It was heavy. It weighed him down with constant worry. It was not easy walking around with his future looking over his shoulder, especially as his life was starting to take shape. His sleep had become broken and disjointed; marred by unremembered nightmares that left a residue of dread every morning.

The proposal and Honey's acceptance had been a big step for him. It was the one decision he did not question. He knew it was the right move. He knew it in a way he couldn't explain in words. His marriage, his family would be the foundation upon which his new life would be built.

III

"Mike, Mike, wake up." It was Honey. Her voice was terrified as she shook him awake. "You're sweating in your sleep, are you ok?" He woke with a start, still trembling, and went to the bathroom. He splashed cold, bracing water on his face.

"Are you still thinking about jail?" Honey asked from the doorway. His face was blank. All he could do was stare. He felt like he wasn't there at all.

"You know what? Let's go," said Honey. "We have enough money saved, we'll wait for things to cool down and come back afterwards."

"Leave here? Right now? Are you sure this is what you want to do?" He was still trying to shake the sleep from his brain.

"Yes, I'm sure Mike. I love you. Let's pack all our stuff and leave, just me and you," she said. Mike was convinced she'd do anything for him, and his heart swelled at the thought. It was powerful. It made him feel strong.

He thought it over, going back and forth, weighing the options, the pros and cons. He finally decided she was right. It would be best if they left. He didn't want to go back to jail. He wanted to leave, but he was reluctant to take Honey with him. He knew that he trusted her completely, but he wasn't sure if she could survive a life on the run. He knew it wouldn't be easy on her and he did not want to put her in that position. But he also knew there was no way he could live without her. His greatest strength was also a weakness.

Mike had $100,000 saved up and that was more than enough for them. They packed up two suitcases of clothes and necessities. They didn't want to take too much. They didn't even know where they were going, let alone what they needed. This wasn't the first time Mike had had to run. In 1999, right after the strongarm robbery case that eventually landed him in prison, Mike had fled. Back then he was inexperienced and scared, and prone to mistakes. He was ill-equipped to deal with an underground life. He had no money and very few connections outside his own, small world in the neighborhood. He only lasted five months that time. He had learned a lot from that experience. This time, having money with them would make all the difference. Having Honey by his side would be a huge advantage, even though there was a certain amount of risk in bringing her along.

The decision was made. Mike knew it was their only option.

Chapter 4: On the Run

I

The first thing Mike did was call his parents and tell them he was leaving for good. At first, they tried to talk him out of it, but his mind was made up. He knew he could trust his parents. They were reluctant, but they eventually promised not to say anything. He told them he would call them when the time was right. They knew the police would be looking for Mike, so they concocted a story that Mike took off; no one knew where he was, no one had heard from him for days.

They had to lie to Honey's parents. They only knew Mike as a real estate agent. They knew he made good money and made Honey happy, but that was all. They knew nothing about his other life or his past. They told Honey's parents they were moving because they had found a cheaper house and New York City was becoming too expensive. They explained how they wanted to get out of the crowded city and live a simpler life. It was all a lie and it worked. Her parents supported the idea.

Mike was relatively safe from the police at Honey's parents' house, at least for a little while. Not many people knew they were together, only immediate friends and close family. It was a good place to stay out of sight while they planned their next moves. They cut ties and tied up whatever loose ends time allowed them. Mike found it easy to erase his presence from NYC, like he had never been there. It made him stop and wonder what he had been doing all this time.

Honey was more rooted in her life. She had a close circle of friends, a lot of extended family in the city, and a good job. Mike knew he was asking her to give up a lot. Up until the very moment they got in the car to go, Mike was certain she was going to bail on him. Fear had built a scenario in his mind where Honey refused to go with him at the last second, and in the days leading up to their departure it was all he saw in his stress-fueled dreams. It would have broken him if she refused.

To his relief, Honey remained steadfast and true, like she had since day one.

Mike thought it would make sense to dump all the money from his account into Honey's. They had yet to combine bank accounts. Mike knew that once the police realized he was on the run they would freeze his accounts. Mike also owned two cars at the time: an Avalanche and an Acura, both in his name. He knew that the police would be looking for his cars. He sold the Acura, and with that money he bought a new Maxima and put it under Honey's name. He drove the Avalanche to a secluded spot and left it there. After that, he went on a spending frenzy maxing out all his credit cards. From now on he would have to pay for everything in cash.

This also meant that Honey had to change her life for him. She wouldn't be able to see her family and friends. She could still visit if they were careful, but it would only be once or twice a month. Honey was an insurance broker. It wouldn't be too difficult for her to transfer.

The last thing Mike did was write all the important contacts in his phone on a piece of paper, then broke his

phone and threw it in the trash. He knew they would try to track him through it. They hopped in the Maxima with the clothes on their backs. They had no idea where to drive until Mike said: "Upstate, let's go Upstate. I have a cousin who lives in Syracuse, it's quiet there."

"Ok," replied Honey.

"We can go to a cheap hotel for a few nights and figure out what we are going to do from there."

Mike wanted to go Upstate because he didn't want to leave New York. He knew that if he left, the charges he would face would only get worse. Going Upstate was the safest thing to do and the best place to start a new life. He also had a real estate deal that was about to close in a few weeks. The profits would be big, somewhere around $50,000. They wanted to stay close until the deal closed. Both knew that every decision they made had to be very precise and they could not afford mistakes.

"Are you sure you want to do all this just for me?" asked Mike.

"Yes, I'm sure. It was my plan in the first place. I'm here for you, Mike, and I would hate to be away from you. I know that you are so much more than a criminal. I see the softer side of you."

"The softer side?"

"The side that understands that there is more to life than negativity. I see a person who has changed and is trying to do better. Whether you see it or not, I want you to know that *I* see it and I'm willing to help you become that better person."

Mike was speechless. The only thing that he could say was: "I love you, Honey."

"I love you, too. Now, let's get through this," she said.

They got in the car and Honey began driving. They were praying they didn't get pulled over. Honey kept her eyes on the road and avoided speeding. Mike turned on the radio and looked for something upbeat. They tried to distract each other from the legal trouble they faced, Mike making silly jokes, trying to get her to laugh. They pulled over to get gas and use the restroom. Honey got them some snacks but neither of them were hungry. Mike never thought he would be doing this, he never saw himself in a situation like this, but he also felt immeasurably lucky that he was with Honey. Mike wanted to give her a rest, so he drove the rest of the way to Binghamton. His adrenaline was high. He told Honey that if they got pulled over, their story would be that Honey didn't know anything and was just along for the ride. Mike was making phone calls and checking messages when his lawyer called and left a voicemail, telling him they were supposed to have the pretrial ready and they needed to know where he was.

Mike looked at his blowup phone and said: "Fuck it,

it's done." They stopped at a Walmart where he smashed the burner in the parking lot. He went inside and bought another prepaid phone. He was happy that he didn't have to constantly worry about court and parole office visits every week. For the first time in months, they both felt calm and relaxed. And even if it was only temporary, it was still better than the inaction of fear and anxiety. Just to be moving was like being able to breathe again.

They drove for two more hours and stopped at a hotel. They planned on staying for a couple of days. The first night, Mike felt less stressed about the situation and felt more secure about it with Honey by his side. When they woke up, they got breakfast from the diner across the street. They ate in silence. They agreed to only talk in the hotel room or in private. Once they were back in the room, Mike mentioned that it would be a good idea for them to get a small apartment. They wanted to normalize themselves as much as possible.

For the next few days, Mike looked for an apartment. He had no luck finding anything suitable, so he called his cousin, Anthony, for help. Mike knew that if he wanted to stay hidden, he would need help from the people he trusted. Anthony didn't understand why Mike would want to leave the city. The only reason Anthony was up there himself was for a job.

"So, why are you here again?" asked Anthony.

"It's a long story," answered Mike. He didn't know if he should tell Anthony. He just wanted help finding an apartment. He also knew it would be better if Anthony understood what was happening.

"I got time," said Anthony. "Tell me everything."

"I got caught up with a drug charge and broke my parole. They tried to give me five years. I've been in and out of jail too much in my life. I just want to enjoy my freedom. I have a strong feeling that I was going to wind up incarcerated again. We decided to make a run for it. We've been up here for 4 days now, trying to find a place to live. All I need from you is to help me find a place to stay. Something temporary where I can lay low." They debated whether Mike and Honey staying permanently would work out. Anthony thought it would be a good idea for them to move around. Mike thought that it would be smarter if they found one place and blended in as much as possible.

After a lot of searching and legwork, they found a place to stay, and it was much cheaper than the hotel. They would put it in Honey's name. She had to show proof of income. Everything went smoothly and the landlord didn't question them much, he didn't even seem to care why they moved. It wasn't ideal, but they were happy to have their own place. Honey decorated to make it feel more like a home. It didn't feel like they were on the run. It felt like they were playing house – a nice, normal couple just trying to live and be happy. They knew they couldn't let their guard down.

For the first couple of weeks, Mike didn't even step outside the house. He stayed home while Honey went to work. Her company had an office not too far from the apartment, and she slid right in without missing a beat. They were excited and completely in love with one another. They watched movies, cooked together, and fell deeper in love. Their strained and frenetic lifestyle gave them unique insight into each other's personalities. They were facing pressures most "normal" couples would never know, and while heavy and exhausting, this pressure solidified a bond that was already strong into something formidable, something almost holy.

Since Mike didn't have to report to his parole officer, he started smoking weed again. His thoughts were now focused on money. He knew he had to make money. He tried the stock market, which he had a natural instinct for, it seemed. He looked into selling things on eBay. He was trying to sell off some of his clothes.

People upstate were vastly different from people in the city, and they had a different sense of fashion. They were quiet and not flashy at all. He noticed that some of the best-selling items were cars. He thought of the Avalanche he left in the city. He knew he could sell the Avalanche but wasn't sure how he would get it. He couldn't ask Honey because she was busy working as much as possible. He asked Anthony. Knowing Mike's situation, Anthony eagerly said yes. Mike told Anthony where he left the car. He told him that if it wasn't there it was in police custody. Mike secretly expected it to be gone, but, surprisingly, it was there. Anthony got the car back to Mike. Within a week Mike was able to sell it for a profit. He realized cars were in high demand upstate because there was very little public transportation. He came up with a plan to buy and resell cars. He already had a hookup, and he knew that he would be able to buy cheap cars from Florida. He could sell them for double what he paid. It took off quickly, to Mike's surprise, and he found himself importing cars with quick turnaround. Once he was up and running, Mike was moving systematically and with great ease. He did this for a few months, fastidiously sacking away every penny he earned. He was building a nice-sized emergency fund. Money was the key to their freedom.

It did not take long for them to settle in and establish a routine. Mike was cautious. He was gently schooling Honey in evading the police. They would prepare for situations. Mike would drill her several times a day about what to do, how to act, if certain scenarios arose. If the cops came looking for him, they had a code: if Mike called Honey, she would say a sentence with the word "veal" in it. If Honey said "veal" it was a red flag. They had a meeting point set in case they ever got separated. It was down in Miami.

Everything was going great until Honey got homesick. She missed her life back in the city. She was able to visit, but it wasn't enough. She wanted more. He didn't want her to feel bad or have second thoughts about the relocation. He was willing to do anything to make her feel comfortable. Mike was afraid this would happen. He began showering her with gifts. He took her out more, regardless of the risk. He knew that spending time together was what she really wanted.

"I'm just not feeling this place anymore," she said. "It's just me and you all the time. It feels like a lot is missing. Maybe we should get a dog."

"A dog? Ok, babe. Anything you want. We'll go first thing in the morning, you can get any dog you want."

"I was also reading a book," she said. "It's a story similar to our situation. They ended up having a kid so that people would see them as more of a family."

"So, you want a kid?"

"Yes, I would love to. I just feel it would be the next step in our relationship, but if you're not ready for that responsibility, it's fine."

"No, let's do it." Mike said.

"I think it would amplify our love and help us blend

in more as a family. People would see you as a father; as a part of a family rather than an individual."

"Cool, but I think we should start with a dog first and see how everything goes."

Even though he knew he'd be the one cleaning, feeding, and walking the dog most of the time, he didn't care. The next day they went to the kennel to pick out a dog. Honey was overwhelmed with joy. The dog that caught her eye was a Maltipoo. She was perfect for Honey. They named the dog Daisy. Daisy made Honey very happy, but Mike knew that it would only be temporary. He wanted to find something more permanent for her. He felt as if she were giving more to him than he was giving to her.

For the next two months, Mike and Honey tried to have a baby, but no matter how hard they tried, Honey wouldn't get pregnant. They took a trip to the hospital, and the doctor prescribed prenatal vitamins and supplements.

II

Mike used money from the stash he had accrued to buy a house. It would be more comfortable, especially for a dog and, eventually, the baby they were planning to have. After a few months they found a place that was in their price range. Mike knew the house was a great deal, and he knew all repairs and work needed would be relatively simple. The house was nondescript and located on a quiet, verdant street. Tree-lined and manicured and utterly indistinguishable from any other neighborhood, it would be easy to hide in plain sight here. It was perfect. This was a step up for them. They had their own space and more room to move and grow. The house had a patio and a pool, which Honey really liked.

Mike planned to do the repairs himself. He and Honey took trips to Home Depot to get the tools and materials they needed. They were just like any other young couple starting their life, there was nothing suspicious about them whatsoever, and they both began to feel a lot safer and freer. The other suburbanites never even gave them a second glance. They hardly warranted a first glance, let alone a second. Mike was getting out of the house more and looking over his shoulder less.

They were excited about their new home and wanted to throw a housewarming party. They settled into a domestic routine: Mike would make breakfast in the morning, Honey would go to work, and Mike would take care of everything around the house.

He smoked weed and played video games all day. In a matter of months, he became a different person. He had never really played before until Honey encouraged him. She had bought him an Xbox so he wouldn't be bored, and he became hooked on it. Online gaming took up a lot of his time. He became friends with the people he played. He was able to interact with people while keeping his identity secret. Anthony would come over and they would play video games, eat, and smoke together.

Mike had been getting his weed through Anthony. This became very time-consuming for Anthony because Mike was buying small quantities often and it made for more trips, more communication, and more risk. Plus, it was kind of a pain in the ass for Anthony to make a run every two or three days, so he suggested Mike buy in larger quantities. It made more sense financially. Mike agreed, but Anthony wanted Mike to come pick up the weed instead of delivering it. Mike knew that was a bad idea and refused.

"Yo, come on, it's just this one time," Anthony said.

"One time is all it takes."

"Are you seriously that paranoid? If anything was going to happen, it would've happened by now. Plus, the cops here aren't as hard as the cops in the city."

Mike was against it but eventually agreed. He took out a suit and hung it in the back. "If we get pulled over, we tell the cops we're going to our uncle's funeral," Mike said.

"You're paranoid," Anthony said, laughing.

They drove 20 minutes until they reached a gas

station. This gas station was full service. The attendant walked up to the car and asked: "How much do you need?"

"A full tank and a half pound," Anthony replied as he handed the man a wad of money. The man began to pump the gas and then went back into the station. He came out with a black bag and handed it to Anthony, who then put the bag under the seat and drove off.

"See, it's as easy as that," Anthony said, coolly.

"Yeah, great. Now, let's get home."

As soon as they pulled out of the station, red and blue lights flashed in the rearview mirror. They panicked. Anthony looked at Mike with complete shock. If the cops found the weed in the car, Mike would go back to prison for sure. He was hoping that the car didn't smell of weed. They pulled over and were silent. They could hear the police officer's footsteps as he approached them.

"Funeral, right?" said Anthony.

Mike was speechless. He just nodded yes and looked forward. He didn't even want to make eye contact with the cop. Anthony took out his license and registration.

"Gentlemen," the officer greeted them. "You were driving 10 mph past the speed limit. Are you in a rush?"

"Yes, we are, we actually have…" was all Anthony could get out before the officer spoke over him.

"Rush to where?"

"We're going to our uncle's funeral and we're

running late. We barely even had time to change for the occasion." The officer looked inside the car and noticed the suit hanging in the back. He nodded to himself and said: "I'm sorry for the inconvenience, drive safely." Before Mike could open his mouth, Anthony began apologizing.

"I'm so fucking sorry, man. I should've listened to you. I could've gotten you in serious trouble."

"Just drive me home," said Mike. He was too rattled to be angry.

They drove home in silence. Anthony pulled in front of Mike's house and tried to apologize again. Mike couldn't believe he almost risked his freedom for a half pound of weed. He walked in the house and said nothing about it to Honey.

III

Honey's parents wanted to visit. They were becoming more insistent and inquisitive about the situation and wanted answers. It wasn't easy for her to lie to them. It didn't come naturally to her, and it didn't sit well on her shoulders.

A housewarming party would be an ideal time to clear their suspicions and help with the homesickness. It had been more than six months since they had gone on the run, and they both missed their families terribly. On the day of the housewarming Mike and Honey cleaned the house and cooked special Asian dishes. It felt good to work together as a team. They were nervous and excited and couldn't wait to show off their beautiful new home. Mike's family arrived an hour before the expected time.

"Mike, how are you?" His mom opened her arms to hug him.

"I'm great. Honey and I have been maintaining and living way better than we were before."

When Honey's parents came, everything was casual. They didn't ask too many questions. They were quiet. They chatted with Mike's parents for a little while and enjoyed the food in a low-key manner. They had brought some gifts for the home: a gorgeous new silverware set, some fresh cut flowers, and a favorite photo they had put in a beautiful, ornate frame. They didn't stay long. Honey's parents left, hugging her and Mike goodbye and wishing them all the best. Mike's parents sat at the table. They had some dessert and talked and laughed together. They were all happy to be in each other's company. Mike's dad said goodbye and gave everyone a hug. He went to start the car while Mike's mom helped them clean the table and wrap the food. She put both of her hands on the sides of Mike's head and looked into his eyes.

"Please take care of yourself, and Honey, too. I love

you so much and only want the best for you both. Please call me if you need anything, me and dad and Amy are always here for you." She had tears in her eyes, but Mike could tell she was holding back and trying to stay strong. He felt guilty about the situation he had put everyone in because of his actions. Looking into his mother's eyes was difficult. She gave them both a hug, kissed them on their cheeks, and said goodbye. It was a sweet, sorrowful scene. Mike was held in her gaze for an uncomfortably long time, and he felt her eyes searching every corner of his soul. He could never hide things from his mother.

After everything was finished for the night, Mike and Honey felt relieved. They didn't have to lie. They embraced in the living room, looking around at their spotless new home. It was so beautiful, and they were glad to see their family and share their home and a small part of their life together with them. It had been such a good day. They were content.

The only thing missing was a child. Mike could tell how badly Honey wanted to be a mother. She didn't say anything, she didn't have to. It was evident in every aspect of her essence. He could see it in her eyes, he read it in the long, unprovoked sighs she uttered. He could feel the emptiness between them; the missing. They had been trying for months and Honey was still not pregnant. They decided they would give it more time before going back to the doctor.

A few weeks later, Mike was in the living room playing his game when he heard Honey scream from the bathroom.

"Mike! Guess what?" He got up in a hurry, startled.

"What's wrong? Are you ok?"

"I'm pregnant!" There was a brief flash of quiet in Mike's head as everything dampened down to silence. Warmth and relief crept over him. He could feel the joy in her voice. It was infectious. His face lit up as he hugged and kissed her for several minutes, both crying. It was the closest moment he'd ever had with her; with anyone, for that matter. Every defense was stripped away, every bit of anxiety left their bodies in a physical sensation. This was the most vulnerable Mike had ever felt in his life. It was powerful. It was scary. Calm and quiet came over them. Mike felt his life change in that silence. As the tears rolled down his cheeks, he knew this was it. This was real life, and this was his chance.

He held Honey tight. She was clinging to him with force. Mike's head swam. Instances of his life came rushing up in violent memories, vivid pictures in his mind of the man he was. He took a deep breath, and in their shared silence, their bond grew and strengthened.

Chapter 5: Settling In

I

"Do you think it'll be a boy or a girl?" asked Honey. "What should we name him or her? I can't wait to see what they'll look like."

Mike was just as excited as Honey. Her happiness was inspiring. It was light, airy, and exactly what Mike needed. They had no idea what to expect. During the ultrasound they were able to see the baby in her womb. They stared at the screen in amazement. Honey teared up while Mike held her hand. They ran a few more tests and were able to determine that Honey was at 11 weeks. She was healthy and strong, and the baby was in great condition.

"So, is it a boy or a girl?" asked Honey.

"It's too soon to tell the gender, but the baby is extremely healthy from what we can see so far," replied the doctor.

"Those prenatal vitamins must've worked," said Mike.

"Do you smoke or drink?" asked the doctor.

"No," said Honey.

"Good, you keep taking those vitamins and your pregnancy should be a
breeze."

When the doctor mentioned smoking, Mike knew he would have to slow on his habit or stop for good. Honey and the baby were his top priority.

"Is there anything we should be on top of?" Mike asked the doctor.

"Honey, just be aware of how your body feels and come in for
regular checkups every other week," the doctor replied. While he was talking, Mike was taking mental notes of what to do. He would be with her at every doctor visit. They didn't know if they should tell their parents yet or keep it to themselves for the time being. Mike contacted his parents, and he couldn't hold back his excitement. He spilled it five minutes into the conversation. They were shocked but happy. They were willing to support them through the next couple of months.

Honey's parents were going to be a different story, though. Honey was afraid of what their reaction would be. She was reluctant to tell them. The thought of letting them down brought discomfort to her heart. She was still unsure how they felt about her moving away with Mike. When she finally got the courage to tell her parents, it was nothing like she expected. They joyfully accepted the news and were genuinely happy. Honey was relieved.

Now that she was pregnant, she had to tell her parents that she was getting married. Her parents wouldn't allow her to have a child if she wasn't married.

"Mike, we're gonna have to front like we're married so my parents support and approve of us having this baby."

He looked at her quizzically. "Huh?"

"Yeah, you can rent a suit and I'll buy a cheap wedding dress. We can take pictures in front of a church and everything."

"Are you crazy?" Mike said, laughing.

Honey laughed. "No, I'm serious!" They looked at each other and cracked up.

"Okay," Mike said. "What do you want to do?"

"We can go to David's Bridal. They have cheap dresses there."

"Okay, when?"

"How about now?"

She was anxious. By now Mike knew every nuance of every gesture, every tic, every nervous characteristic; like the endearing way the left corner of her mouth twitched almost imperceptibly when she was vexed. Their time together under such extreme circumstances had forged a bond so symbiotic that Mike, at times, felt like he was inside her head. He smiled a little while watching her go through the outward machinations of a tense decision. He wasn't even aware he was doing it and she caught him.

"What's so funny?" Her lower lip pushed out in a defiant, child-like pout. "Why are you laughing at me?"

"I'm not laughing at you."

"Yeah, that kind of doesn't work when you have a giant smile on your face while you're saying it, jerk." She was softening.

Mike was full-on beaming. Just looking at her made his heart swell.

"I just love you," he said, shyly. She ran to him and threw her arms around his neck.

II

It was a crazy plan and Mike did not think it would be convincing, but off they went to buy a real wedding dress for their fake wedding. Honey was awash in the nervous excitement of buying her wedding dress. Even while accompanying and abetting a wanted fugitive, every girl still dreams of their ideal wedding dress…

They got to the shop, and she was jumping out of the car almost before Mike could even put it in park. She ran to the front door. She was blushing and could barely contain herself. They walked inside together and were greeted by an older woman.

"Hello," she greeted them. "How can I help you?"

"We're here to try on some dresses!" Honey exclaimed. Her exuberance caused Mike to turn his head.

"Well, she is, not me," Mike said. They all laughed.

Honey and the sales associate walked around looking at dresses while Mike waited. Honey came running up to Mike with some dresses in her arms. She went into the dressing room. A few moments later she emerged, looking stunning in a beautiful wedding dress. After all the searching, this was the one. Mike was floored. He had never seen Honey look so beautiful. He was speechless.

"How much is it?"

"It's $1,500 and we will hem it for free."

Honey and Mike both looked at each other. They told the saleswoman that they would be back and thanked her for her help. As they were ready to walk out, she made a last-ditch effort and offered them the dress for $1,000.

"Maybe we should just buy it," Mike said. "It looks beautiful on you."

"I don't know. Feels like it might be bad luck to buy it without a wedding date. Let's go home and think about it."

They were having a baby and couldn't afford an expensive dress. They settled for one less expensive. Mike wanted to give her the one she really wanted, and it broke his heart to have to tell her they couldn't afford it.

He was gutted. They planned to do it big and have a real wedding one day when the time was right. At this point they were just trying to keep Honey's family happy and, more importantly, to keep them from getting suspicious.

Mike contacted some old friends from Canarsie, Yohan, who was engaged to Christine, and Anna. They were currently living in Florida. Anna had one child and another on the way. Yohan's fiancé was pregnant, too. Honey, Anna, and Christine were all due around the same time. The crazy thing was these were the only two people Mike really kept in touch with. He had stopped talking to his friends in New York and focused on his life with Honey. It wasn't just caution that made him cut off all contact with his people. Mike recognized this as a turning point in his growth. If he wanted to move on from the person he had been to a responsible father and husband, this would be a big step. Even if he wasn't consciously aware of it in the moment, some part of him knew. And from that knowledge a new bit of resolve grew within him. It was small, imperceptible; almost invisible. It was just a vague feeling told in signals that he was just learning to understand.

There comes that time in a person's life where they find completion, and their isolation with that person is a compelling force. For Mike it began and ended with Honey. He knew he had to leave that life, and if that meant leaving behind his closest friends then that's what he had to do. Again, these were not conscious thoughts in Mike's head yet. Just the deep, undefined rumblings of adulthood.

Mike took Honey shopping for baby stuff. They did not know the gender yet, but they went all-out anyway. Most of the stuff they got was bright yellow.

"Babe, we're having a baby not a duckling," Mike said. They laughed.

Honey said they needed unisex colors for now, so yellow and white were the main choices. Mike bought a few blue items anyway and Honey picked up some pink things. Over the next few weeks, life was idyllic. Almost normal. Honey didn't really throw up much or have any severe pregnancy symptoms. They ate healthier, home-cooked meals and less fast food. Honey went to work, and Mike sold cars through a small, online enterprise using auction sites. Honey was barely showing, and she wasn't going to tell her job until the baby bump was visible.

Soon it was time for the next sonogram, and this one would tell them the baby's gender. Mike wanted a boy, but knew he'd be happy either way. Honey didn't care at all, as long as the baby was healthy. The doctor moved the ultrasound tool around Honey's belly at different angles.

"I don't see a penis," Mike said.

"You are correct. Congratulations on your baby girl," the doctor said with a smile. Mike was elated. He hugged Honey.

"It's a girl, Mike!"

"Yes, it is, and she will be beautiful just like her mother." They hugged and waited for the doctor to come back with the pictures of the sonogram.

"I can't believe it's finally happening," said Honey. "In a few months we'll have a small version of ourselves."

When the doctor bought back the sonogram pictures, Mike stared at them in amazement. He couldn't believe that he had a baby on the way. Now that they knew they were having a girl they went to work. They turned one of the rooms in the house into a nursery. They painted the walls pink and arranged everything until it was perfect. He could see Honey's enthusiasm and mirrored it with his own. It was genuine and these were the memories that Mike kept forever.

Their days were spent going back and forth from Home Depot, Target, Babies R Us, and a host of other stores getting ready for the baby's arrival. Unfortunately, Mike was beginning to feel the financial squeeze. His online auction sales had slowed, and he needed a new plan. His first thought was to start flipping houses again, but that was going to be difficult. He wouldn't be able to put anything in his name. He decided to try the stock market. He had made money before in the stock market and knew that if he put more time and effort into it, he could make a lot more.

He got some books, read stock blogs, watched videos on You Tube and immersed himself in any bit of knowledge he could find. This was right as the market was coming out of an early-2000s crash. Things had been bad for a while, but now that a recovery was slowly starting to build, Mike thought it was a good time to jump in with both feet. He would study the market, watch financial shows every day just to get knowledge. While he had no formal training whatsoever, Mike was a natural hustler, and his instincts were honed and sharp. His skills translated easily from one hustle to the next, and really, there was only one rule to the market: buy low and sell high.

Honey was skeptical. She felt like it was a scam and that it was a set up designed to take advantage of people. But she trusted Mike and even with her misgivings and trepidation, she was willing to go along with this venture.

In the first two weeks Mike did well. He wasn't back to his usual earning yet, but it was a start. He was buying stocks in the hundreds and making small profits. With some shrewd and bold gambles, he made $40,000 in 3 weeks. He sold as soon as possible and deposited the money into Honey's account.

"Honey come look at this," Mike called to her when she came home from work. "I just made $40,000!"

"I knew you could do it. Let's put the money into a

savings account for our daughter," Honey suggested.

"No, I'm going to invest more. I have a feeling we could get rich off this."

"We should invest hundreds instead of thousands,"

"Can you just trust me? I know what I'm doing."

"I'm afraid you're being greedy." She was worried.

"I'm not being greedy, I'm being ambitious. I believe in chance and opportunity. This opportunity has fallen into our laps, and I think that we should make the most of it. It takes money to make money."

"I think you should just listen to me for once." She was getting upset.

"Cool," Mike said in sarcastic exasperation. He felt she wasn't backing him on a decision he felt very strongly about. The sudden silence created a heavy tension. Honey went straight for the bedroom, and they didn't speak the rest of the night.

III

After a few days, things settled into a tenuous peace as the functions of home and life forced them to work as a team. Mike spent time pondering Honey's wishes, and it was with some apprehension that he decided to take her advice. He kept the budget in the hundreds. It didn't last long. Much like a gambler in the throes of their addiction, Mike was motivated by the hustle and the compulsion was getting stronger. He needed to take bigger risks because he needed bigger, faster rewards.

The temptation to up the ante was too much, and that's exactly what he did. He invested $40,000 into another stock. The stock dropped dramatically. In the span of a few days, he discovered the company had gone bankrupt. The stock was worthless, and he was unable to sell his shares. He hoped there was money left over from the firm's liquidated assets to pay the shareholders, but there was nothing. He regretted his decision. The stocks flopped. He had no idea how he was going to break the news to Honey. He was sick to his stomach with guilt and utter bewilderment. His confidence was shaken. He was forced to question everything, every decision, every move he had made. In his previous life, this kind of hesitation and doubt could cost far more than money and Mike worried that his instincts were being dulled. There was fear; a panic in his throat and chest he had never experienced.

It didn't take long for Honey to notice $40,000 missing from the account. The bank contacted her to let her know the account balance had dropped significantly. She was furious.

"Mike, what the hell happened to the money? I thought I told you not to do anything with it." She was fuming.

"I kinda fucked up," Mike said softly without looking at her.

"'Kind of?' Mike, that's $40,000 down the drain. I don't get it, I thought we had an agreement. How could you go behind my back and do something like this? I thought we were a team?" Her voice was rising, she was shaking with anger.

Mike was speechless. He knew he was wrong. Dead wrong.

It took time, but eventually they settled their dispute, and everything was smooth. Honey's pregnancy took precedence over everything else, and Mike tried his best to keep his focus narrowed on the only thing that mattered: being a good father.

Before they knew it, Honey was 7 ½ months pregnant. She was granted paid vacation from her job. She used her sick days to stay home. They decided to have a planned delivery and scheduled it for April 10, which was Good Friday.

When the day came, they went to the hospital excited and nervous. They broke Honey's water around 10. She was in labor for nine hours. She was pushing, screaming, and squirming while Mike was by her side.

"It's gonna be okay, you're doing great! I am here for you," Mike said. She hadn't taken any painkillers because she had been worried about the side effects. The first time she started pushing, nothing really happened. The pain kept getting worse. Mike could see that she was struggling.

"Maybe you should try the painkillers, babe," Mike said. She looked at him and nodded. They gave Honey the epidural and within minutes she calmed down and everything was fine. It was easier for her to push. The doctors put her legs up in the air and told her to breathe along with a bar graph that was beside the bed.

"I can see the head," Mike said. Honey's face reddened as she pushed. He kept telling her to breathe. Before they knew it, Honey was holding their newborn baby in her arms. She was crying and breathing heavily with exertion.

"Mike, we did it! Look at our daughter," Honey said, panting.

"She's beautiful, just like you."

Their reverie was interrupted by a nurse telling them, "As the parents we need both of you to sign off on these papers. Have you picked a name yet?"

Mike immediately froze. "No, we haven't thought of a name yet," even though they knew what they were naming the baby.

"Take the baby home and you can send the forms to us. You have a week to submit them."

Mike waited for the doctors to stitch Honey back up. The doctor took the baby to weigh her.

"She weighs 6lbs. and 15oz. 20 inches. She's healthy and beautiful. Are you going to breastfeed?"

"Yes."

"You're going to have to do it right now if you want to start breastfeeding," the doctor said. He handed the baby back to Honey and showed her how to breastfeed. "Do you have any questions or concerns," the doctor asked.

"No, I don't. I'm good for now."

Mike's mom walked into the room to check on Honey and met her new granddaughter. "She's beautiful. I'm so happy for you!"

"Thank you."

After the breastfeeding, the doctors checked to make sure the baby was in stable condition. Everything was great and he gave them the go-ahead to take her home. Mike slowly wrapped her up and handed her to his mom. She showed her to Mike's father. Honey called her parents and told them the good news. They were excited and happy for her. They were unable to make it to the hospital, but they promised to come visit and spend time with them as soon as possible.

Mike's parents stayed and gave them a hand. His mother understood they were new parents, and she was willing to help them any way she could. She and Honey became closer. She taught Honey about some of the mysteries of motherhood that she had mastered. Mike watched his mother dispense tender instructions the way only an experienced mother could, and he marveled at what was a tradition as old as humanity. In an odd way he felt so connected to lives lived and lost over the course of thousands of years, and he felt a swell of pride in his chest thinking about his daughter becoming a part of that chain of history. Just watching Honey hold his daughter was life. He was surprised at how heavily the emotion hit him. He was not prepared for it. The simple gestures of motherhood were outlined and drenched in symbolic meaning for Mike. The tableau before him was holy.

Honey only had a few more weeks of paid vacation left. Even though his mom was helping a lot, Mike knew he would eventually have to step up and help more. Once his parents left and Honey went back to work, he would be the one taking care of his daughter. He still couldn't believe he was a father. He knew that he wasn't just living for himself anymore. He was responsible for another life. That thought settled onto his shoulders squarely and it felt right.

Honey's parents came to visit. They still had no idea that Mike was on the run. They also didn't know he was unemployed. They thought he was still working in real estate. While they were there, he would leave the house for hours to make it seem like he was working. He would go to his cousin's house, or he would hit the gym. Mike was sure her parents didn't care for him. He knew that if they ever found out the truth it would cause all kinds of static and tension. The situation was harder than he had anticipated. He began to overthink *everything*. He couldn't get a job and he felt the pressure of keeping up appearances for the sake of Honey's parents.

When Honey's parents left, Mike told her their situation wasn't ideal for their daughter. He wanted to move to another state. He told Honey the house wouldn't be profitable to resell because of all the money they had already put into it. His plan was to move and rent out the current house. Mike felt it was time to move on.

They still hadn't submitted the paperwork to the hospital, and they hadn't picked a name for their daughter yet. They had it narrowed down to two choices: Myah or Mariah.

"Myah. I love that name more and more every time I say it. Mariah also has a ring to it," she said.

"I think Myah is a beautiful name," Mike responded. They got up and stood over the crib to look at their sleeping daughter.

"Myah is a beautiful name, and she looks like a Myah," said Honey.

"So, Myah it is. Myah Joy." They had named their

daughter.

Mike's fugitive status prohibited him from putting his last name on his daughter's birth certificate. It also meant that he would have no custody over Myah until he was able to get his situation cleaned up. The possibility of not having custody of his daughter hurt Mike worse than he could imagine. There was nothing he could do but strengthen his resolve and forge ahead with his plans.

A month passed and Honey went back to work. Mike would have to go full daddy mode: feeding, cleaning, playing, and taking care of Myah's every need. Everything went well at first. Myah began to feel the difference between the bottle and Honey's nipple and refused to drink from the bottle. She would cry frantically, and Honey would have to leave work to come home and feed her. Mike was constantly unsure and worried, and it made him feel like things were getting out of control. Myah would not eat unless Honey was there to feed her and nothing Mike tried worked. He wanted to see if Honey would be allowed to work from home, this way she could help him with Myah.

"I don't think they'll let me do that," she said. "Besides, I've already been missing a lot of days. I'm sure they would say no. We have to figure something out."

"Well, I still think you should ask. The worst they can say is no. You are one of their best workers, I'm sure that they would understand." He was desperate for help.

"I'll ask tomorrow."

The next day Honey came home with a huge smile on her face. "They said yes!"

"They did?" Mike was surprised.

"They told me I could work from home and that I would just have to come into the office once a week to check in and update them."

"This will make everything so much easier."

Mike got a call from his friend Yohan telling him he just got a job at a car dealership in Jacksonville, Florida. Mike had mentioned that he was looking for a new place to live and Yohan suggested they move down to Jacksonville. Mike told Yohan that he would have to ask Honey.

"Honey, how would you feel about moving to Florida?"

"Florida? Why would we go to Florida?" she asked. She was confused.

"Yohan told me he just started working at a dealership, and that he'd be able to get me a job there. Plus, I don't want to stay here for too long. What do you think?"

"If that's better for us then I guess we should do it."

"Okay, cool, I'll call Yohan and ask if he can help us move and find a place. We need a change of scenery. We would have to tell your job that you're moving and would have to work from home all the time."

"Mike, I think that they were being generous by letting me work from home in the first place. I think asking that would be too much."

That night, after they put Myah to bed, they went to their room. It had been a very long day for them. Mike put his arm around Honey, and they sat in peaceful silence for a while.

"If we're gonna be on the run we're gonna just have to adapt and be like a military family until we figure something out and get a lawyer to help with this. I don't want to get too comfortable and be stationary, so this move is going to be a good decision right now," Mike said.

Mike's previous lawyer had said something that had really stuck with him. He said the longer the case ran, the better. Mike wanted to stay on the run until the statute of limitations ran out. It was a long shot, but he and Honey had already been doing this for a year and a half. Now they had a baby, a house, and a dog. He felt confident that if he stayed cautious and followed his instincts, he could beat it out.

Mike contacted Yohan and told him they would need help moving. He wanted to bring their car and a moving truck, but the drive would be too long and risky for him to drive that far. Mike agreed to pay for Yohan's plane ticket to New York and then Yohan would drive down to Jacksonville the same time as Mike and Honey.

The following day, Honey came home with a huge smile on her face.

"They said yes. I had to bend the truth a little bit, though," she laughed.

"What did you say?"

"I just told them you got a job offer in Florida and that you needed to

leave as soon as possible. They told me I would have to check in by phone three times a week and as long as I'm still doing my job and things are running smoothly, everything should be just fine."

"Good. In a few days Yohan will be on his way here to help us pack and move everything, so let's get everything situated." They began putting things in boxes. They packed up everything in the living room. They wrapped the couches. The living room became a storage area for everything. Mike put the house on the market.

A day before the move, Mike's parents made a surprise visit.

"Happy 100th day, Myah!" Even though it was unusual, they celebrated the 100th day of Myah being alive. It was a Korean tradition, dating back to the war. A lot of the children born then didn't make it. Every day they survived was celebrated and counted as a blessing. It was a ritual that was important to their generation. Mike's parents came with presents and joy but were confused once they saw all the moving boxes.

"What's going on?"

Mike explained: "We're going to Florida. We need a better place to raise Myah and we don't want to stay in one place for too long."

They didn't say anything. They knew the situation. His dad grabbed an empty box and put the gifts he bought for Myah in it. "No need to open this now. You guys need help packing?" he asked.

"Yeah, everything in the kitchen needs to be packed up and we're going to start throwing away the food that we aren't taking." By the end of the night, most of the apartment was packed.

The next day Yohan showed up bright and early, ready to drive. He took a

cab from the airport and hopped right in the U-Haul. Mike and Honey got in their car with Myah and started driving.

IV

When they reached Florida, Mike and Honey encountered a situation. They were moving into a gated community and as soon as they drove in, there was an old white man staring at them. Mike didn't want any problems, so he didn't pay him any mind. But he knew that look, and he knew what it meant.

"You can't park there," the man said with an air of authority.

"Why not? Me and my family are new here, we are about to move in." Immediately Mike's temper rose, but he knew he had to keep everything under control. The neighbor told Mike he had to park the U-Haul outside the gated houses and then bring his things in, which would be a lot of extra work.

"We're almost done, just a few things left," Mike was saying in a conciliatory tone, trying to calm the situation before they called even more attention to themselves.

"I don't care. I am the president of this neighborhood's Homeowners Association, whatever I say goes," the man said petulantly. "Do you want me to call the cops?"

Mike didn't want to start any trouble, so he just took everything out of the truck as quickly as possible and brought it into his new home. The altercation worried Mike because he wasn't even doing anything wrong. It took everything within him to stay cool, but once the situation calmed down Mike was left to think about how differently he would have handled things before Honey and Myah had become his life.

Mike had family in Miami, and even though he and Honey had just moved to Jacksonville, he was already thinking of moving to Miami. Their first encounter with

Jacksonville hadn't gone so well, and it had left Mike concerned that more situations like that would arise. He felt that the people in Jacksonville were racist, and Honey and Mike being Asian didn't help much. Miami was a bigger city than Jacksonville and Mike thought they would feel more at home there. It was a much bigger city, and it would be easier to blend in and go unnoticed. Jacksonville felt like another prison. Miami felt like another chance.

Chapter 6: Welcome to Miami

I

Mike and Honey once again packed everything that they had and hit the road. Mike drove the moving van and Honey drove the car with Myah and Daisy in the backseat. They would be able to blend in and it would be an easy transition since Miami was similar to New York in many ways. They rented a small apartment in a nondescript complex and signed a six-month lease. The lease would help prepare them to buy another house in a better part of Miami. The plan was to live in a good neighborhood for Myah. They wanted to give her the best education possible. They couldn't afford private school, so their goal was to move to a good district for school. They moved to Miami because they loved that it was always sunny, the beach was right there, the people were beautiful and nice, and the atmosphere was more city-like. Even though Miami was only a four-hour drive from Jacksonville, the scene and the vibe were vastly different. People were always dressed in beach attire. They stopped at Walmart for a bathroom break and some food. Everywhere they looked women were half-naked.

"Why are all these women dressed like this everywhere we go?" Honey asked. "Do they not have any respect for themselves?"

"Baby, it's Miami. That's the norm down here," Mike replied.

"Yeah, I can see that, but there are still children around and it wouldn't hurt them to cover up." Hearing Honey's reaction to the women of Miami planted a seed in Mike's head. He knew to watch his eyes and be aware of how he was interacting with women. He loved Honey and never had any thoughts of cheating, but he couldn't help looking.

After they packed the house and settled in, Mike went outside to get some fresh air. As soon as he stepped out of his apartment, the scent of weed hit him. It had been a while since he smoked. As he turned around and looked to his left, there were two Jamaican men smoking and talking. Mike wasn't usually into making new friends, but he needed to figure out where to get weed. He began talking with the two men, telling them he just moved in with his family from Jacksonville and how he was from New York, but liked the weather in Florida better. After going back and forth about Mike's transition from New York and what they all did for a living, one of the men offered the blunt to Mike.

"My name is Rob, by the way."

"I'm Mike."

The two dapped each other and continued their conversation. This was the first time in years that Mike smoked with or spoke to anybody he didn't know well. After a few pulls, he was feeling a nice high.

"Where'd you buy this from? This is some good weed," Mike said.

"I sell it," Rob replied. "You looking to buy?"

"Yeah I am. I usually buy in large quantities, but let's start with an eighth and go from there."

Rob nodded, reached into his pockets, and gave Mike the weed. Mike looked at the weed before handing him the money. "How much is this going to run me for?"

"$40." Rob paused for a moment before he continued. "But I'll give it to you for $35." Mike handed him the money. As he walked back to his place, Rob yelled to him: "I'm guessing you just moved into the only empty apartment. I live two doors down from you. If you like what you got, come and knock on my door, I'll be home."

A couple of days later Mike knocked on Rob's door. "Yo, you got that? This time I'm gonna need a half," Mike said.

"Of course, just come in real quick." As soon as he was inside, he noticed a whole bunch of music equipment.

"You rap?" asked Mike.

"Nah, I don't. I'm actually a full-time DJ at a club out here in Miami. I just sell weed on the side for extra money," Rob explained while handing a tightly rolled sandwich bag full of aromatic buds to Mike. "You should come out one night. The clubs here are crazy. We always have people vacationing, so people are always just letting loose and getting wild."

"Nah, I'm not really the party type anymore." Mike mentioned that he knew people that DJed in New York, and that the parties up there were also pretty wild.

"I always wondered what DJing was like in New York."

Mike and Rob went back and forth on several different topics that branched off throughout their conversation. They ended up talking for an hour and a half, smoking and chilling. Mike didn't expect it, but he ended up making a new friend. He wasn't going to tell Rob about his situation, but he felt like Rob was someone he could trust. He chilled and smoked with Rob often.

Mike and Honey became more comfortable with Miami. Myah was getting older and developing fast. They had her in her walker for a while each day to strengthen her legs, and in no time, she was up and walking. This gave Myah more freedom to roam around the house and she would spend most of her time chasing Daisy around. She would play very roughly with Daisy, pulling her ears and tail, and climbing on top of her. Even though Myah was a menace, Daisy never retaliated. It was like she knew Myah meant no harm. She would always stay by Myah's side no matter what she did.

They knew that if they wanted Myah to excel, her education would need to start from home. Mike would read to her and try simple arithmetic. Honey did the same when Mike was out selling cars.

Mike would scour auction sites looking for deals. The market was far more active in Miami, so the cars were cheaper. He would ship the cars back to Jacksonville and make anywhere from $2,000 to $5,000 a car.

They enjoyed parenting and spending time together as a family. His car hustle was going well and having some steady income helped ease the financial tension he and Honey felt. She was still a little gun-shy from the $40,000 loss, but she had more faith in Mike's car hustle than the stock market, so she worried less. Mike rode his bike to the gym three or four times a week and spent lots of time with Myah.

One day at the gym, he noticed a woman staring at him. She looked familiar. He didn't know if she was attracted to him or if she knew something about him. He racked his memory trying to figure it out when it finally hit him. She was an old friend of Honey's. Her name was Rebecca, and Mike had seen her at the barbecue where he first met Honey. From a distance, she waved at him with a big smile on her face. Mike waved back hoping that would be all. He put his head down and continued to curl his last set of dumbbells. Just as he finished, he felt a tap on his shoulder. As he looked up, there was Rebecca with a huge Kool-Aid smile on her face.

"Don't I know you from somewhere? Weren't you dating Honey? You're Mike, right? Honey's boyfriend? You guys totally went M.I.A. Is this where you've been this whole time? Why did you move?" She peppered him with a barrage of questions. He knew she was just being friendly (if a bit nosey), but he still felt like he was being interrogated.

"Yes, we live here now," Mike said in a low voice.

"Me too, I work at this gym."

"I come here all the time. I don't see you," said Mike.

"I just started."

He could tell by the way she was talking that she

knew nothing about his situation, and that made him feel more at ease. He was no longer in a rush to leave the gym. All he had to do was act natural. He continued to talk to her as if his life were completely normal.

"Where's Honey?" she asked. He almost told her they had broken up. He knew it wasn't a good idea. What if they bumped into her together? He thought about it and decided Rebecca wasn't a threat.

"She's at home with our daughter."

"Daughter? Honey has a kid, and she didn't tell me?" Rebecca was shocked.

"Yes, we have a daughter, her name is Myah. She's about 14 months now." Mike showed her pictures.

"She is so adorable! I have to see her in person. Honey and I have so much catching up to do." She grabbed a pen off the information desk and wrote her number on the back. She insisted on seeing Honey and gave Mike her phone number.

"I'll make sure she gets this." Mike said and left the gym. As soon as he got home, he told Honey about what had happened. He wasn't sure how she was going to take the news.

"Babe, guess who I saw today."

"Who?"

"Do you remember Rebecca?"

Honey's face lit up with joy. "Rebecca from

Brooklyn?"

"Yes, she wanted me to give you this." Mike took the piece of paper out of his pocket and gave it to her. She immediately dialed the number. She seemed happy to reconnect with her friend. Even though Mike was cautious about it, he didn't say much. Honey rarely got a chance to enjoy herself. She made plans to hang out with Rebecca. This was perfect timing because Mike's sister had just made plans to come to Florida to visit. Amy was so busy with work that it was difficult for her to get out of the city, and a trip to Miami to see her niece had been long overdue. She had also enrolled in medical school, which made Mike proud. He was excited to see her and looked forward to her visit.

A few days later, Amy arrived. On her first day there she wanted to go to the beach. It was 103 degrees, and it was perfect beach weather. Mike picked her up at the airport. She was happy and smiling. It was good to see her. Comforting.

"I missed you guys so much," Amy said, hugging them both.

"We've missed you, too."

"You must be Myah," Amy grinned while picking her up and making funny faces. This was her first time meeting Myah and she was beyond ecstatic to embrace the little bundle of energy that was her niece.

"You're the spitting image of your dad," Amy said to Myah. As they drove, Amy took in the scenery and repeated the same thing Honey had said when she first arrived in Miami: "So, do all the women here just walk around in bikinis all the time? I understand it's hot, but wow." Mike was silent and pretended not to hear.

When they got home, Mike quickly hopped out of the car, grabbed Amy's bags, and ran up the steps. By the time everyone else got upstairs, Mike was coming from inside the door saying he'd be right back.

"Where are you going?" Honey asked, using her hand to dramatically stop the door while she walked inside.

"I'll be at Rob's crib, give me 10 Minutes."

Amy unpacked her bag and was ready to go back out in the sun. For her, being in Miami was a vacation from New York and medical school. She just wanted to enjoy herself. Honey packed some lunches and loaded everyone up with sunscreen. She packed the car and put Myah into her car seat.

As they drove, they spoke about Mike's situation. Mike was ready to lie and make up a story. It was as if he was talking to a stranger, but he realized that he was talking to his sister, who knew everything. It became the norm to lie about his life to people. His lies were a defense mechanism so ingrained that they were automatic. Mike had been on the run for 3 years and he was living a good life. It got to the point where he believed his own lies and, in the moments when he was confronted with the actual truth, it was unnerving and disconcerting. It was a jolt back into a reality he was subconsciously avoiding.

After an awkward silence, Mike said: "I think moving every three or four years is a good plan. I want to be comfortable." Honey was quiet. She didn't like to speak about their situation to anyone but Mike. It made her uncomfortable, too. That was another reason Mike didn't mind Honey rekindling a relationship with Rebecca.

"Amy, guess who I'm speaking to again," Honey said, changing the subject.

"Who?"

"Remember Rebecca?"

"Rebecca? From Brooklyn? I haven't seen her in ages," Amy replied.

"She lives here in Miami, too. Mike ran into her at the gym. She works there. We're going to hang out tomorrow, you should join us."

At the beach, Mike played with Myah in the water until he got tired. He ate and then promptly fell asleep. While he slept, the women played with Myah in the water and built sandcastles and enjoyed the beautiful day. It was so peaceful that it was easy for Mike to forget that he was a wanted fugitive and that he and his family were on the run. It was easy to fall right back into that other reality, where he was a normal father taking his family to the beach. It was easy and comfortable.

With things going so well with his family, he had started to allow himself to think about the future, something he had never really done before. The thing was, Mike found himself wanting this quiet family life for real. He hadn't even realized how badly he wanted it. With Myah, his priorities had shifted dramatically. Before it had been about pure survival for him and Honey. He hadn't had time to think of anything deeper. Myah had changed everything. It wasn't her fault that her father had fucked up, and she shouldn't have to pay the price for it. She was innocent and deserved the best life possible. He wanted to live in this world permanently. It was something that ached inside of him, and it made him angry that it was such a struggle. Mike had lived in the lie so long that it had acquired some truth. This *was* his life now, and it was a life that suited him. It was the life he wanted.

II

Mike and Honey went house hunting in Miami. Mike wanted to get out of the apartment complex. They felt Myah needed a proper home, a house to grow up in and a yard to play with her dog. They were just about to leave when there was a knock on the door. They looked at each other, confused. The only time anyone knocked on the door was when they were expecting a delivery. It couldn't have been Amy because she had left two nights before. They waited a few seconds, and the knock came again, louder.

"Who is it?" Mike asked.

"It's me," a voice said.

"Me who?"

"It's me, Rob." Mike opened the door and greeted him. It was a little weird because this was the first time that Rob had knocked on his door.

"Yo, there is this big event going on at my club tonight. You should come," Rob said.

Mike glanced over at Honey and said: "I told you, I don't party or go out much anymore. That's not my scene. I'd rather just spend time with my family."

"Yo, just one time. Plus, I'm DJing."

"I think you should go," Honey said. Mike turned around, surprised. He already knew she felt uncomfortable with the woman in Miami. He couldn't understand why she wanted him to go to the club without her.

"It's been a while since you had some fun on your own. I think you should go."

"Cool, I'll see you tonight. Be ready by nine," Rob said. Mike couldn't think of anything to say. He wasn't even sure he wanted to go.

"Cool, I'll be ready," Mike said.

"I'll take you on my motorcycle," Rob said, heading out the door. "I have an extra helmet."

They went to meet an agent to look at houses. Mike didn't want to mix business with friends, so he contacted listing agents of properties that were listed. It made the deals easier dealing with one agent None of the houses they saw seemed right for them. Either they were too big, too small, or the school was too far away. They wanted to live in the suburbs.

Once they got home Mike got ready to hit the club with Rob. At 8:55, Rob knocked on his door.

"Yo, you ready Mike?"

"Let's be out." Turning to Honey, he said: "I'll be back soon, do you have everything that you need, babe?"

"Yes, I'm fine. Go enjoy yourself."

This was the first time in a while that Mike went out socially without Honey. He was just going to have a few drinks, party, and go right back home. Mike put his helmet on and hopped on the back of Rob's motorcycle. The line outside the club stretched around the corner. Memories of Mike's old life came flooding back. He thought back on the days before Myah and Honey, before he was on the run. The days when he was completely reckless. He could do anything he wanted with no regard for repercussions, at least until that landed him in prison. He felt like he was starting to slip a little. He felt like he was getting a little too comfortable. He deserved to go out and have fun whenever he wanted and being isolated all the time wasn't something he had to do. It also wasn't healthy for him. He could go out whenever he wanted. It was a risk, but one that seemed more appealing than being locked away at home afraid of being arrested again. He wondered if it were possible for him to go out and have fun and still be able to control himself.

They were only a few feet from the club when Mike realized that he had forgotten his ID. Before he could say anything, Rob hopped off the motorcycle and dapped up the bouncer.

"The Asian guy is with me," Rob said. The bouncer nodded his head and made way for Mike to come through. Once they were in the club, everyone was feeling good. Rob ordered a few bottles and began pouring. Mike took a few shots and started dancing with women. He felt free. He didn't think about his situation, he wasn't worried about making money, the only thing on his mind was having a good time. Two hours of drinking, dancing, and laughing went by when he heard screaming. He looked over and saw Rob throw a drink at some guy. They guy claimed Rob had stepped on his shoe. Mike made his way over there and without even thinking knocked the guy out in one punch. The crowd gasped. Another guy stepped to Mike. He turned, threw a punch, and buckled the guy's knees. He slumped and fell.

Mike was disappointed in himself. He had started the night with good intentions, but now he was angry with himself for being unable to control his impulses. It took him years to create stability and build a family, and he had just risked it all. He knew that he made bad decisions sometimes, but he usually always had good intentions. In an instant his future flashed before his eyes. All he saw was Myah's face.

Someone yelled: "Call the cops!"

Mike grabbed Rob and ran out of the club. They hopped on the motorcycle and took off. Mike could tell Rob was still drunk by the swerving of the bike. They were only two blocks away from the club when they looked back and saw the cops pulling up. They had narrowly escaped. Just seeing those red and blue lights made Mike's heart race with fear and adrenaline. All he could think about was making it home safely to his wife and daughter. Once they pulled into the parking lot, Mike hopped off the bike while Rob was trying to thank him for having his back.

"Yeah, it's no problem," Mike said, fumbling to find the key to open his apartment. He wanted to get away from Rob and into the safety of his home as fast as possible. He went straight to his bedroom and saw Myah in Honey's arms. They were both sound asleep. He took a deep breath and thought to himself: *I have to be more careful with my life. I'm living for more than just me.* He went to the bathroom, showered, and slept it off. The next morning, he said nothing about his night. When she asked how it went, all he could do was exhale, shake his head, and say: "I'd rather spend time with my family than go clubbing."

Chapter 7: Self Love

I

After the unfortunate event at the club, Mike decided to stick to his weekly routine of work, gym, and home. He wanted to move as soon as possible. He felt like he had attracted negative attention. He didn't want to be out with his family and be recognized by anyone who had been at the club that night. Being a 6-foot hood Asian made him stand out, and every time he went out, he felt like everyone was staring at him. He could tell that Honey was irritated and wanted to get out of the small apartment. Because of his real estate background, Mike knew the houses he was shown weren't worth their asking prices. Honey suggested they move back to New York where they knew people and had connections. Mike knew this life on the run was taking a toll on her. He could see the exhaustion in her eyes, the worry on her face and, as much as he loved her and needed her, he knew this was no way for a family to live.

"We can be extra careful with what we do and where we live," she was saying.

"Why would I move back there?"

"I didn't say move back to New York, I just wanted to move closer. Maybe like New Jersey or Connecticut. We don't know anyone here. We have to lie about everything. I'm just tired of hiding all the time." Mike didn't say anything.

She understood why he wanted to stay in Miami, but she felt like she had sacrificed her whole life for him. She did everything in her power to make her life normal, but it was still hard for her. She felt guilty for resenting Mike. She knew how much he needed her. When she had decided to go with Mike, she never envisioned how her life would change. Being on the run was not easy on her, as both a wife and new mother. She missed her family and friends. She felt isolated. She loved Mike, but she wanted her old life back. She wanted Myah to grow close to her friends and family. She wanted her to have a diverse experience, immersed in different perspectives and personalities, and to develop healthy bonds with a solid support system.

"Let's try one more agency and look at a couple more places. If we don't find anything, we'll move," Mike said after a long period of silence. Honey agreed. The rest of the ride home was silent.

At home, Mike began scouring the Internet for houses. He found a two-family duplex for sale, with someone living in one half of the house. The realtor was looking for a family to move into the other half. Mike was skeptical but still called to schedule an appointment.

Mike and Honey were impressed by the house. It was a joint house. It was spacious, with two bedrooms, a nice-sized kitchen and two bathrooms. It had a backyard with a small, built-in playground that was connected to a bigger community playground. Mike envisioned a small privacy fence around his playground.

Mike managed to talk the realtor down to a lesser figure. It was a steal. Although Honey wanted to move from Miami, she also wanted this house. They bought the house and moved in immediately. They bought new furniture and remodeled the rooms. They threw themselves into the project and working together was fun. They laughed, had late nights of bad takeout and painting parties, talked about their hopes and dreams for Myah and for their future.

II

They were still receiving rent money from the house

in Upstate New York. They were in a comfortable space and didn't have to worry too much about money. Mike thought they should buy another house to rent out for more income.

They looked for another house but didn't have much luck. Mike was more passionate about buying and selling houses than Honey was. Honey was taking trips to New York more frequently. Her parents wanted her to come to New York with Myah for Thanksgiving. Mike did not want them to go without him, but he gave in because he could see how important it was to Honey.

Mike stayed in Miami to work and to look for houses. With Honey and Myah gone he felt like a part of him was missing. It was the first time he had been away from his daughter since her birth, and he did not like it. He had never expected it to be this hard.

By Monday morning Honey had stopped answering her phone. Mike was afraid something might have happened to them, and he called her parents. Her mother told Mike that Honey and Myah were going to be staying there for five more days. Mike understood why Honey would want to stay, but he was upset she didn't tell him herself. He felt he was losing her and that one day she was going to leave and not come back. Doubt began to creep in and erode his confidence.

When they returned to Miami, he picked them up

from the airport and greeted them with hugs. The extended trip took a toll on Mike. He hadn't slept or eaten well the entire time they were gone. He loaded their bags into the car and Honey drove them back home.

Five minutes into the drive, Mike said: "Don't you think it was kind of selfish to not tell me you were going to be spending extra time in New York? You didn't answer any of my calls or texts and I was worried that something had happened to you guys."

Honey lashed out, "Sometimes I just need a break from this life. It's not always about how *you* feel or what *you* want. What about me?"

Mike was about to argue, but he understood what she meant. "What do you want me to do?" he asked. "Things don't magically just get better."

"You never take what I want into consideration." He could hear her anger rising.

"Well, if you spoke up more instead of having these temper tantrums we could communicate better." Mike was getting very agitated.

She breathed deep and looked Mike directly in the eye. "You're selfish. All your care about is yourself. You barely pay any attention to me anymore. You're a great father. I also think you're a great husband. It's just this situation… it's killing us."

"What do you mean by '*us*?' Who is '*us*?'" Mike's

voice raised.

"It's killing *me*. If we don't find something better soon, this will affect Myah, too," she said.

He knew she had a valid point. If he were to turn himself in it would ruin everything he had built over the past few years. Now that they had Myah, everything was different, and that had to factor into every single move he made.

When they got home, Honey stormed out of the car and went straight inside the house, leaving Mike and Myah outside. She said nothing to Mike. A few hours later she apologized for lashing out. She was overwhelmed. Mike wanted her to communicate more. They had acknowledged their grievances but hadn't found resolution, and it hung over them. They argued over trivial things for weeks. Mike tried to get out of the house more frequently. He was irritable, and his irritability was easily enacted with the slightest provocation. At times he was petulant, sullen, and uncommunicative. He spent more time at the gym and at work. He was working hard, even though the car business was slow. He wanted to make sure he could provide for Myah in case he got caught. He was starting to think about emergency plans in case he had to go back to prison. He didn't want his family to struggle financially if something happened to him. He was also spending a lot of money. He was used to having nice things and he would sometimes spoil himself. He bought himself a BMW 745 Alpina White with 22-inch rims. There was some hesitancy, as it was a very flashy car, and he was trying to stay low-key. He got such a good deal that he couldn't refuse. But, in the back of his mind, he knew he was playing a dangerous game. He was trying to make himself feel better by spending money, but the effects were temporary, and the guilt came soon after.

One day, while he was driving to the gym, he pulled up alongside a car that was being driven by a young Spanish guy. He looked 25 or so. He had car club stickers plastered all over the vehicle. When the guy saw Mike looking at him, he revved his engine, wanting to race. Mike was a block from the gym and uninterested in racing. The light turned green, and the car sped off. Mike went at his normal pace. Within seconds, cop lights flashed and both cars were pulled over. Mike looked at the cop and pointed his finger at himself, mouthing the question "me?" through the window. His heart dropped to his stomach as he pulled over. He thought of driving off but decided against it. Mike knew that he was going to get in trouble. He pulled over, scared.

The cop went to the other car first. Mike texted Honey. When he looked up, the cop was writing a ticket. He handed it to the other driver and sent him on his way. Mike's mind was racing. His palms were sweaty. Honey had texted him back. Before he could even open the message, the cop knocked on his window.

"License and registration, please." All business.

Mike looked at the officer. "I don't have the registration for this car because I have a temporary plate for it. It should be good for another week." He hoped the cop wouldn't ask for his ID.

"What about your license?"

Mike hesitated and looked in his wallet for a few seconds, pretending that he couldn't find his ID. Talking to himself out loud he said: "Did I bring my license today? Did I forget it at home?"

"Why would your license be out of your wallet?"

Mike whipped out his fake military ID and handed it to the officer. His heart was pounding, and his nerves were fried. He tried to seem as calm as possible. He had memorized all the details on the ID card and knew that the officer would question him about being in the military.

"So, you were in the military?" the cop asked, trying to intimidate him. "What rank were you?"

Mike knew the cop was testing him.

"I was a lieutenant, sir."

The cop asked a few more questions rapid-fire. When Mike had gotten the fake ID, he had spent a day with a friend who had been in the military learning enough jargon to get through a mid-level interrogation.

"I have a lot of respect for people who served in the military," the officer was saying. "I'm going to let you off this time. Drive safely."

Mike had no idea why he was pulled over. He said to the cop: "Can I ask why you pulled me over?"

"Because you were going 4 mph above the speed limit. I thought you were about to race the other driver," the officer said. Mike didn't say anything else. He waited for the cop to pull off. He sat there for a moment and looked at the messages that Honey had sent him, along with 3 missed calls. He read the texts.

Mike, are you okay? Please call me back as soon as you can. He called Honey and told her everything was fine and that he would be home in ten minutes. He drove home and decided that he wouldn't drive that car anymore. He wondered if he had been pulled over because the car stood out so much. He decided to sell it and buy something less conspicuous. He listed the car and got a response from someone in North Carolina. The guy sent him a $500 deposit.

Feeling better about getting rid of the BMW, Mike took Honey and Myah to see a movie and get dinner. It was raining. It was the first time he had driven the car in the rain.

"The rain is coming inside," Myah said.

"No, it can't. it's not possible," Mike replied, fearing

the worst.

"Look," she said, pointing to the sunroof. He looked up and saw water leaking through the sunroof. He didn't understand how it happened. Everything was getting wet. By the time they got home, the upholstery was soaked. He pushed back the sunroof and noticed there was a crack in it. It was a big problem. The buyer would be there in two days, and Mike was determined to sell the car. They dried the inside of the car and put a thin layer of crazy glue in the crack, hoping that it would stop the leak.

Mike met up with the buyer at a nearby gas station so he wouldn't know where Mike lived. The buyer looked at the car for ten minutes and didn't ask many questions. He wanted to go to the bank as soon as possible to deposit the check. They finished the paperwork at the bank, and the check was written out in Honey's name. Once the bank clarified that the check was good, the buyer left. Mike hoped everything was great and that he would not hear from him again.

III

Mike had to draw the negative attention away from him. He asked Honey if there was a way to remove the tattoo on his neck without surgery. They found something called "the block." It was a cream that, when rubbed into the tattoo, made it go away. He tried it for a month, and all he had was a sore neck. He found a place to get the tattoo removed with surgery. He made an appointment and they accepted him right away, which surprised him. They said there would be seven sessions once a month. It would be $80 dollars a session and he could start right away. He was scared but committed. The tattoo did not represent who he was now. The removal would be symbolic of his transition to the new person he had become.

A few months went by, and Mike found out that the neighbors who lived in the attached house were moving. Mike thought it would be a good investment to own both houses. He could sell them when it came time to move again. He contacted the realtor, and it was a short sale with little negotiation. They closed within six weeks, Mike already planning the renovations. Two weeks went by, and the neighbors still had not left. Mike went over to see what he could find out. Mike knocked and a man answered. Mike could see inside the house, and it did not look like he had any intention of leaving.

"When are you leaving?" Mike asked.

His neighbor replied: "If you pay me, I'll leave faster," and closed the door in Mike's face. Mike was infuriated. He banged on the door.

"Open this shit up or I will fuck you up! Get out of

my fucking house!"

Silence.

Mike knew he wasn't going to open the door. He was playing a really twisted game with Mike, and Mike wasn't having any of it. He went back to his house. Ten minutes later there were cops knocking at his door.

"Yo, are you fucking kidding me?" he whispered to Honey. He ran to the bedroom. They knocked again. Honey opened the door a crack.

"Is your husband home?"

"No, he stepped out."

"Do you know when he'll return?"

"I'm not sure. He's running errands."

"We'll be back."

Honey closed the door and went to the bedroom. Mike could tell she was surprised, scared, and annoyed. She looked at Mike and said: "This is enough. I'm tired of living like this. What did you do now, Mike? It's always a problem with you. Do you have to start problems with everyone?"

Before he could respond she cut him off, yelling: "I don't want to hear any of your excuses."

The situation with the house had caused a rift between them. It turned out that the neighbors had planned this scheme all along. Honey didn't want to deal with the stress, but Mike wanted the house.

Mike said nothing and left. He went to the gym to blow off some steam. For the next couple of days, Honey and Mike argued continuously over the smallest things. She didn't speak to him unless she needed to. Weeks went by and she still didn't change her attitude. Their home was a minefield of tension and long, drawn out sighs. The longer it went the harder it was for Mike to break the silence. Mike only heard her voice when she spoke to Myah.

One day, Mike stepped outside and saw the neighbor. They glanced at each other uncomfortably. He stopped for a second, not wanting things to be more awkward than they already were. Mike half-waved to him. The neighbor looked confused and hurried back indoors.

Mike and Honey called the bank to see what they could do about this situation. They hoped to get a refund. The bank confirmed the neighbor was not leaving. Because of this, they could get their down payment back. They were still within the thirty-day grace period, so the refund was simple and easy. The beef between Mike and his neighbor was squashed. Everyone got what they wanted.

Even with the resolution of a potentially volatile living situation, little had changed between Mike and Honey. The atmosphere was still heavy and cold. It felt like they were only together for Myah. Even though they lived in the same house and saw each other every day, they were disconnected. Mike tried to apologize. He did things for Honey to try and lighten her mood. Nothing worked.

Myah's birthday was coming up and Mike invited his parents to come down from New York. Even they could tell something was off. Honey didn't speak at all. She barely looked at anyone. She stayed in the bedroom and would only come out if she needed something. When Mike's mom tried to talk to her, she was rude and sullen, giving only terse, monosyllabic answers. He took Honey aside.

"What are you doing? My parents came all the way from New York and you're giving them the cold shoulder and making things awkward for everybody."

"*I'm* the one making things awkward? What would your parents say if they knew why I'm so pissed?"

"Listen, this isn't about you right now. This is Myah's birthday. My family is here. You can be pissed at me, and you don't even need to talk to me, but at least keep it together for Myah and my parents. Don't be so selfish," Mike said, raising his voice.

"*I'm* selfish? Mike, do you have *any* self-awareness whatsoever? I already know you're going to say it was my idea to run, but I never thought you would be so foolish and risky with the decisions you've made. I've fucking had enough of this. This isn't a life. Don't you ever feel like you're still in some type of prison? That's what it feels like for me. I feel completely fucking trapped. The only part I played in this was suggesting we leave. Every dilemma that followed was your fault. I've just been along for the ride. I gave up my whole life for you. You don't seem to appreciate it at all. So, who's the selfish one?" Her voice overpowered Mike's. The argument escalated into screaming. Mike's parents tried to break it up and that just made everything worse. His mom mentioned that Myah could hear everything and that they needed to stop. Mike and Honey moved the fight into the bedroom and lowered their voices. Everyone in the house could hear them. Mike's parents left that night and went back to New York. He was infuriated.

They continued arguing long after his parents had left. The week following Myah's birthday was filled with resentment and vitriol. Their arguing made Myah cry. Mike told Honey she had put herself in this situation and that it was her fault she felt this way. They began verbally tearing each other apart. They didn't feel like a team anymore. They felt like strangers and enemies. The damage was too much. There needed to be some space. Mike wanted to work it out. Maybe they could try counseling. The reconciliation needed to be genuine for it to hold. Mike was sinking. He heard himself saying things to the mother of his child that should never have been uttered. Horrible things. The worst part was he knew she was right. He would never admit it to himself, but he knew. This was his fault.

The next day, Honey left. She told Mike she needed a break from him and from Miami. Mike was numb. He watched her fill a giant suitcase silently and get a one-way ticket back to New York. Up until the moment she walked out the front door without a word, Mike didn't really believe she would leave.

She left.

Chapter 8: Back Against the Wall

I

They had been on the run for seven years. For seven years they had been normalizing this insane fantasy that was their life. Honey was gone, and Mike was left trying to figure out where it all went wrong. It only took a few days after Honey left for everything to really hit him. He kept calling and texting her and got no response. He was anxious and angry. But, more than anything, he was afraid. He called his mom daily to vent. He felt betrayed.

Thinking back on all the good times they had put his mind at ease. No matter how bad it got, he knew he still loved her. She always went with every plan he had and never second-guessed his judgement. She was always honest with him and helped him keep his composure.

Mike saw where he had made his mistakes and he was determined to fix everything for Honey and Myah. Even though he wasn't in prison he was still a prisoner of his past. He was anxious. He knew he couldn't change his reality, but he thought that if he put in an honest effort, he could change his perspective and he could change the way he dealt with things.

He made a six-month plan. The first thing on his list was to sell the things he didn't really need: clothes, chains, watches, jewelry. On paper, Mike was broke. Everything had been put in Honey's name and, with her gone, he had no access to the money. He had some cash he kept around the house for emergencies. As part of his new plan, Mike made up his mind to go on an extreme budget. No spending on unnecessary things. He wouldn't be able to sell cars, which was his best source of income, and he didn't want to go back to selling drugs. He figured that if he called Honey and asked her for some money she would understand and would find a way to get it to him. He also wanted to see how Myah was doing. He was determined to stay strong. He had been through so much and his tribulations had given him more motivation. He wasn't fighting for himself anymore. He was fighting to get his family back. Mike knew that he had to survive, so he had to put himself first. He had dedicated his life to being a father and a husband, and he had forgotten how important it was to take care of himself.

A few days went by, and Mike texted Honey again. This time she answered.

Hey babe, just texting again to see how you and Myah are doing, is everything ok? He typed hopefully.

Yes, she's fine, I'm fine, and everything is ok. What do you want? I told you we want nothing to do with you.

What do you mean we? Our fight has absolutely nothing to do with my relationship with my daughter.

I'm telling you she's fine. What more do you want from me?

I wanted to see my daughter, and I need you to send me $3,000 so that I can maintain myself out here.

A few minutes went by. No response.

He didn't want to keep texting, but the silence was killing him. An hour went by. Still nothing. He decided to call her. The phone rang. No answer. He let a few hours go by and called again. She finally answered the phone and had quite an attitude.

"Hello, Mike. What do you want?"

"Is that Daddy?" Mike heard Myah ask.

"Go to your room, Myah," Honey said.

"Why are you telling her to go to bed?" Mike yelled into the phone. "She asked if it was me. She's obviously concerned and misses me." They argued over who did what to whom and who was not being mature in this situation.

Honey again accused him of being a terrible husband.

"A terrible husband? Me? What kind of wife leaves her husband when he is on the run from the cops? I feel like you just gave up on me. I feel like you betrayed me. It's partially your fault we're in this situation."

"*My* fault? How is it my fault? I'm the one who helped you get back on track. I helped you get your first legal job. I did my best to keep you out of trouble. You lied to me by doing everything I told you not to do."

Mike couldn't think of anything to say.

"Can I please talk to my daughter?" he said through clenched teeth, trying to sound as calm as possible. Honey was about to say no, but she could hear the hurt in his voice.

"Myah, come here. Your dad wants to speak to you."

"Daddy!" Myah was overjoyed. Honey felt bad about keeping her away from her father.

"Hey, baby. How are you?"

"I'm good. Mommy said that we're staying in New York for now. When are you coming to visit? I miss you," she said.

"You'll see me soon, Myah. I promise." Mike spoke to his daughter for a few more minutes before Honey interrupted them.

"Okay, Myah. Say bye to Daddy, it's time for bed."

"Bye, daddy, see you soon!"

"Bye, Myah. I love you! I'll call you later."

Honey took the phone from Myah.

"Thank you for allowing me to speak to my daughter. I would like to Facetime with her at least once a day before she goes to sleep."

"I'll let you know," Honey said coldly.

He was just happy he was able to hear Myah's voice. Over the next few days, Mike called regularly at the same time to speak to Myah. It wasn't enough. He wanted her to come see him. Honey still wouldn't speak to him, but she relented because she understood how much Mike loved her and how important it was for Myah to have a father in her life.

Mike was still broke. He felt trapped, and Honey would not give him any money. He called his mom and told her about what she had done. She could tell that something was off. "Is everything okay? Are you and Honey still going at it?"

"Yes, we keep arguing. She took Myah and went back to New York. I don't think she's coming back at all."

"What do you mean not coming back? Why would she do that? Do you need me to come down there?"

"That's actually why I called you. I wanted to see if you could possibly help me out. I'm low on money but I have a plan."

She flew down to Miami. Mike was still heartbroken.

II

While waiting for his mother's plane, Mike heard a child's voice yelling to her father. He looked at the child thinking about Myah and how much he missed her. When he finally saw his mom approaching, he couldn't believe his eyes: Myah was with her. Mike's heart leapt at the sight of her as she called out to him. She let go of her grandmother's hand and ran straight to him. Mike picked her up, crying and hugging her as tight as he could.

"How were you able to bring Myah?"

"Honey said that it was ok. I knew that this would make you so happy."

"I love you so much mom, thank you so much. I am so happy you are here!"

They drove home, got some food, and watched TV together until Myah fell asleep. After she was down, Mike and his mother had a talk about where to go.

"I need to move back to New York. I can't live like this anymore. I'd rather be in New York, closer to you guys and Myah. I'm alone here and all I think about is Honey and Myah. This whole house just reminds me of them every day. I can't live here anymore. I need to get out of here as soon as possible."

The next morning, Mike suggested they sell his jewelry. His mother would have to do it because she had a legit ID. They went to a pawn shop with Mike's jewelry. Mike did all the talking since his mom spoke very little English. He didn't want her to get caught in a lie.

"My mother would like to pawn some of my father's jewelry," Mike began. He started with the watch and the ring only. He didn't want to seem too thirsty.

"Nice watch, do you have the box and papers?"

"No," said Mike.

They haggled over money, and, in the end, they settled on $2,000 for the watch and the ring. He never even asked Mike or his mom for ID. Although it wasn't as much as he wanted, he still felt pretty content with what he got. Mike wanted to celebrate, so they went out to eat. He'd been alone and miserable for almost a month. Having his mom and daughter with him meant the world to him. He told his mom he wanted to go to another jewelry store to sell another watch and a chain. They went to a different store on the other side of town. Mike went in with the same story and came out with $1,800.

Mike wanted to enjoy his time with his mom and Myah. They went out to eat, the zoo, the beach, and the mall. He knew once they left, he would have to go back into grind mode. His mom wanted him to stay in Miami, but he was already set on moving back to New York. He was done in Miami and his life there didn't mean anything without Honey and Myah. Mike's determination reminded his mother of her own father, whom she had lost as a child.

Myah said: "Daddy, I don't want to go back. I miss you. I want to stay here with you."

"Me too, baby. We'll be together soon. I just have to sell this house."

"Don't sell my toys!"

"Ok, Myah. I won't sell your toys."

When it was time to go, Myah said, "Why? I want to stay here."

"I know baby, me too, but let's get ready. We don't want to make mommy upset."

Mike loaded the car with their stuff. It was a very quiet ride to the airport. Myah was already tearing up. Mike parked the car and walked them to the gate. He gave his mom a big hug.

"Thank you so much for everything. I love and appreciate you more than I could ever explain."

"Stay home. Don't go out too much and stay safe."

Myah was crying and Mike's heart broke.

"Daddy, I don't want to go!"

Mike couldn't take it and broke down into tears. He cried as he held his daughter, telling her how much he loved her and that he would see her again soon. He let go of Myah and walked away without looking back. He knew it would be devastating to look back.

He drove home. He resolved to get back into his daughter's life. He was determined to leave Florida. He could not live without Myah.

The next morning, Mike made appointments with realtors to show the house. They listed the house, and within a few days they started getting responses. Two weeks passed, and Mike got a full-price offer on the house. He was excited and knew that he would be out of there in no time. Over the next few weeks, Mike's house was like a garage sale. People were coming by every day to purchase clothes, furniture, toys, whatever Mike listed.

He got a call from the realtor. "We got a closing date! Is next week good?"

"Sure, we can do it next week," Mike said, feeling both excited and relieved. He got off the phone and called his mother.

"You need to book a flight. We are closing on the house!"

"That is great news, Mike! I'm so happy you're coming home."

As the day came for Mike to leave Miami, he began to get cold feet. As his brother helped him finish packing the car, he looked at Mike and asked: "Are you ready?" His brother didn't agree with his decision to move back.

"Yeah, I'm ready."

Chapter 9: Coming Back

I

Mike had so many different feelings and thoughts racing through his mind on the drive back to New York. They stopped in Georgia to get some rest and it gave him a chance to reflect on everything that had gone down. Mike had learned a lot about himself while being on the run. The biggest lesson he learned was that you can only depend on yourself.

Mike was so excited that he wanted to drive until the sun went down. He drove most of the way. He drove all the way to Washington D.C. A few hours later, he called Myah to tell her he would see her the next morning. She was ecstatic. Mike was getting butterflies. They were getting close to New York.

When Mike arrived at his old neighborhood in East New York, it all seemed like a dream. It was a place of many powerful memories. He still couldn't believe that he was back home. His family greeted him with open arms.

For the first two days he stayed in a hotel. Then he rented a room until he could find an apartment. Finding an apartment and getting on a lease was going to be a bit of a challenge, due to his lack of proper ID and paperwork. After weeks of looking, he finally found an apartment.

Mike called Honey to tell her that he got a place close to her. They tried to be civil to one another for Myah's sake. They barely spoke, and the conversations they did have were about coordinating visits with Myah. Things were cordial, they weren't fighting. It was a start and it brought him some measure of peace.

II

He'd been back in New York for two months and was staying low-key. He only spoke to family. He was careful on the phone, he was careful where he went, and he was especially careful while driving.

One day, Mike bumped into one of his old friends at a pizzeria. The guy's name was GS. He and Mike ran together back in the day.

"Yo, Mike," GS said.

"What's up? I forgot your name, but you look mad familiar."

"I thought that was you. How are you doing?"

"I'm good."

"You still talk to Shorty Roc?"

"Nah, not in a while. You got his number?"

"Give me your number, I'll get it to him," GS replied, unlocking his phone to enter Mike's number. Mike was hesitant, but he really wanted to see Shorty Roc. Mike went home. He was nervous about the encounter with GS. He wasn't sure if he made the right decision or not. Later that night, Mike went out for a walk. His one-bedroom apartment made him feel trapped and it was good to get out and get some fresh air. It gave him time to think.

Once Mike got back from his walk, Shorty Roc called him. He gave Mike an address and Mike told him he would be there in a half hour. He got dressed and took a cab to Shorty's. From the back of the cab, Mike noticed they were driving through a nice area. The cab pulled up in front of Shorty Roc's house. As he was waiting, Shorty texted him: *Give me 5 minutes- what kind of clothes do you have on?*

Mike replied to the text: *A blue hat and a blue hoodie, Timbs, and a jean jacket.*

Ten minutes went by, and Shorty still hadn't replied. Mike stood waiting at Shorty's door. He was about to call a cab and leave when a silver BMW pulled up with rims and tinted windows, playing Capone-N-Noreaga's *The War Report*. The driver's side window rolled down, and it was Shorty Roc.

"Yo, jump in, my man," Shorty was inviting him in the car. Mike opened the car door and got in.

"Yo, my bro. I missed you. How are you?" Mike was happy to see him. Shorty signaled that Mike should lower his voice. "Let's not talk here."

A few minutes later, they pulled up to a fancy building. They got into the elevator and went to the second floor. Shorty hit the buttons for two and four.
Mike was perplexed by this.

"Why did you also press four if we're getting off at two?"

Shorty Roc was silent for a moment, then said: "Just in case we got followed."

Mike laughed. "Followed?

"You never know," Shorty replied, shaking his head.

Once they entered the apartment, Mike noticed how clean it was. Shorty Roc had nice furniture, a big screen TV, expensive clothes everywhere: Gucci, Louis Vuitton, Prada, Burberry, Yves St. Laurent, Versace, and more. Mike told Shorty he was happy for him and proud of his success. It had been a while since they'd seen each other, and it was great to be reunited.

Shorty Roc looked over at Mike and passed him a fat and freshly lit blunt. "I'm doing really well now, man," he said, exhaling a huge cloud of pale blue smoke as he talked. "I'm actually in a good position to help you."

"How?"

Shorty Roc took another hit and exhaled a fat cloud

of dank smoke. "Ya boy came up. I'm the plug now."

"Shit, man, that's cool and all, but I ain't trying to get back into the streets."

Shorty shook his head. "Nah, bro, I want you to fix your shit. You're a real one. You could have snitched on me back in the day when you first got knocked, but you took it on the chin and said nothing. That is real shit, my G."

"Thanks, bro. I appreciate it. You know it's not in me to roll over and snitch. It's just not in me." They passed the blunt.

"That's why you need Mitch to get on this, ASAP. He is the man."

Mitch was a well-known lawyer who had represented Shorty and a few of his friends and had gotten good results.

"I don't trust lawyers like that, bro. You know they're the worst crooks."

"You gonna have to trust a lawyer eventually, big bro," Shorty Roc said.

"I guess you're right. How can we trust this one?"

"Oh, Mitch?" Shorty said, taking off his shirt to show Mike a tattoo on his back.

"What is that?"

"His business card," Shorty Roc replied. Mike laughed. Shorty believed in Mitch so much he tattooed his business card on his back.

"Yo, why would you have your lawyer's business card tattooed on your back?"

Shorty had a serious look in his eye as he said: "Because he got my back. He beat a difficult case for me. I was looking at ten years and he beat it. They took 50,000 from me when I got arrested. I got that back, too. Trust me, he is the man. Your case is small compared to mines."

"I'm not sure, bro."

"It's up to you, bro. You've been on the run for a long time. I just want you to be able to chill again, live your life not running anymore. I'm in a better position to help you now. Anyway, let's smoke another blunt. You good?"

"Yeah," Mike replied, trying to process everything he had just been told.

"Aiight, I got some other fire weed we can smoke. Shit gonna get us lit."

Shorty went to the kitchen and was asking Mike questions. "How old is your daughter? Are you and your baby's mom still cool? Why y'all broke up?"

"My daughter is five. Me and her mom are not really on good terms right now but it ain't about us no more. It's about me and my daughter."

Shorty could tell that Mike was still upset so he sparked up the new blunt.

"I put a little wax in it, too. We gonna get fucked

up," Shorty Roc said, laughing.

"Wax? What's that?"

"It's the oils from the weed. You never did wax? Oh, you gonna get nice."

Shorty passed Mike the blunt and he hit it.

"Aiight fuck it! I need to blow off some steam anyway. We need to celebrate. I haven't seen you in years, homie." The blunt was going back and forth in fluid rotation. They continued catching up.

"Looks like you're doing great, bro." Mike told Shorty about his encounters with the police while he was a fugitive. Shorty analyzed everything Mike said. He kept asking questions. Mike was so high from the wax he was almost tripping. Shorty was on another level and had to make sure Mike was still real about his words and wasn't an informant. Mike knew this, knew what Shorty was doing, and understood. He would have done the exact same thing. For another hour, they continued talking about what had been going on in each other's lives. Shorty's stories were about arrests, shootouts, home invasions. It was good to sit and chill. Upon Mike leaving Shorty asked Mike if he needed any bud. Mike said it's cool. Shorty didn't want him driving around copping weed, so he said: "my young boy gonna bring you some tomorrow." The next day, Mike got a text from a number he didn't know. It turned out to be Shorty's friend with the weed. They met up at 77th and

Main. While Mike was waiting, he called Shorty.

"Yo, your worker Young Boy hit me up. He's coming through to drop me some bud. Good looking out, bro. Did you talk to your lawyer?"

"Yeah, I did. We meet him tomorrow." Shorty sounded pumped to introduce Mike to Mitch, but Mike was starting to feel a little nervous and apprehensive about the whole thing.

"Wait, tomorrow? Why so quickly? Why tomorrow?"

"That's when he's good, bro. He got time tomorrow, so just come meet me there. I'll give you the address."

"Are you sure we can trust him, bro?"

"Let's see what he says. Maybe bring $1,000, just in case."

"For what?"

"We might need to retain him. If you don't like what he says, we'll just leave."

The next morning, Mike was nervous about meeting the lawyer. If Mitch chose to take on his case, Mike would pay him a cash deposit up front. At this point, he wasn't sure if Shorty Roc was trying to set him up or not. He couldn't help but wonder if Shorty would give him up and sell him out for his own hidden, selfish benefits. He had to think on all the angles, no matter how improbable they might seem on the surface. His mind was working furiously trying to feel out the situation. He got a text from Shorty telling him to meet him at Mitch's office. They were going to talk to him together. At that moment, he just wanted to call Myah and hear her voice.

"Hey, Myah. It's daddy."

"Hi, dada." Myah was excited to hear from him. Mike felt a lot better after hearing her voice. They talked for a while, and it was easy. It made sense. It was so far removed from talk about lawyers and retainers and shootouts.

After speaking with Myah, he went to meet Shorty at the lawyer's office. He was early, so he drove around scouting out the area. While stopped at a red light, Mike saw a cop pull up behind him. His eyes widened and he began to sweat. His mouth went dry, his heart practically leapt out of his chest. He was scared shitless but kept his cool. He drove the speed limit and knew he just needed to get out of the cop's way. He turned into a gas station and the cop went right on by, barely noticing Mike. Mike exhaled, relieved but shook. He let out a small, weak laugh at himself.

He pulled up to the building and saw Shorty standing outside with a big goon. The guy was a menacing 6'8" and 300 pounds.

"What's good, bro. Who is this?" he smiled at Shorty and nodded towards the heavy dude.

"He's my driver and security man," Shorty replied,

winking at Mike. Shorty may have been a character, but he was all about his business. He knew how to separate the two. Shorty went up to Mitch's office mad arrogantly, acting like he owned the place. He immediately began bossing people around, telling them to bring them some coffee and to go get Mitch. Shorty looked like a Reggaeton guy. Versace glasses, Versace belt, Gucci jacket, Gucci sneakers. His outfit alone must have cost at least $5,000. He had close to $20,000 worth of chains on his neck.

Mitch walked in. He gave Shorty a pound and a hug like he was from the hood.

"What's going on, fellas?" Mitch greeted them. "Mike, I know a little about your case, but I want you to tell me about it and what you want to do."

"Well, my case is about ten years old, and I've been on the run for about seven. I'm tired of running and just want to take care of the situation."

"You haven't had any police contact in all this time? Where have you been the past seven years? How did you survive? Why do you want to turn yourself in now after all this time?"

"Whoa! Wait a second, I barely know you and you're asking too many questions."

Shorty interjected: "Nah, Mike. He's just trying to figure out your best defense. I put my name on it. He's good, bro."

Mike took a minute to gather his thoughts. "I've been hiding under my ex's name, but we broke up. We have a daughter and I just want the best for her. I feel like now is the time to take care of everything."

"I don't think this case is that difficult. It's old and you haven't gotten in trouble since. Let me make a couple of phone calls and see what I can do. What's your number?"

"You can call Shorty. He will hit me up. I'm sorry. It's nothing against you, but lawyers have done me wrong before."

"Yeah, just hit me up. My boy is still paranoid about you," Shorty said, laughing.

"I'm working for you now, so you're going to need to trust me," Mitch said. "I'm going to start working on this tomorrow. Today, I'm gonna need a retainer of $2,500."

Mike looked up at Mitch. "Huh?"

"You got that rack?" Shorty asked.

"Yeah."

Shorty pulled out a knot of about $10,000. He gave Mitch another rack, matching the $1,000 that Mike had just put down.

"Let's do two thousand now, and once we've seen some progress, I'll give you another two."

Mike and Shorty left the office together. "You know I got you," Shorty said, his arm around Mike. On his way home, all he could think about was how relieved he was going to feel once this was all taken care of, and he could finally live his life out in the open.

III

That weekend, Mike took Myah to F.A.O. Schwarz. He had never been there. It was one of the best weekends they'd had together since he'd been back in New York. Mike still wasn't sure if he was going to have to do any time for his previous case. He still owed parole time and figured they would violate him if he took a plea. He was putting all his trust and faith into the lawyer he just hired.

Monday came around and Shorty hit Mike up. "Mitch called me and said we need to come in."

Mike paused for a minute. "Why? Let's call him on 3way, but don't say I'm on the line."

"Hold on, I'll call him now. Put your phone on mute." The phone rang a few times and Mitch finally answered.

"What's good?" Shorty asked.

"Let's talk in person. I don't like to talk on the phone. You and your friend need to come see me. I spoke to the D.A., and he's got it in for your friend. This D.A. is an asshole. I know him. He wants your friend to turn himself in. Then after that, we will work out a deal. That's what he wants."

"But how long has he gotta do?" Shorty asked.

"I'm not sure. Maybe the whole thing? He needs to come here. When you come, bring another $2,000. This is gonna cost some money."

Mike hung up, frustrated that he had just lost a thousand dollars. He took a minute to really weigh out his options. Again, he was faced with another potentially life-altering decision.

The next morning, around 6 A.M., Mike got a call from his mom. "The police just left. They came to the house looking for you."

Chapter 10: History Repeats

I

"Cops? What do you mean? How many? Were they in plain clothes or did they have uniforms?"

"They had regular clothes on. Did you do something? You've only been here for a few months and suddenly there are cops at the house looking for you. You really need to be extremely careful with who you talk to, Mike."

After Mike hung up, his first thought was that it must have been Mitch who called the cops. Mike wasn't sure if Shorty Roc was involved, or if it was someone else completely. His mind was racing. He wondered if it was smart to trust Shorty Roc. He wondered if Shorty was the one that turned him in. Maybe Shorty had something going on that Mike wasn't aware of. Mike was completely shook and confused. He needed a minute to think things out. He sat in his apartment the entire day wondering if he should text Shorty and let him know what happened. He decided that this was a conversation that needed to be had on the phone. He would be able to hear Shorty's voice and see if there were any cracks. He called Shorty.

"Yo, the boys came to my mom's crib today."

"How did they know you were back in New York?"

"Honestly, I'm kind of thinking Mitch lined me up or he just made me hot."

"Nah, he wouldn't line you up, bro. Let me call this dude right now."

Shorty called back a few minutes later and told Mike he needed to smash his phone and get a new one. Mike went and got a burner. He called Shorty back. Shorty wanted to meet up at his place. Mike knocked at the door and as soon as he walked into the house, he found himself in a huge cloud of dank weed smoke.

"I screamed on this dude, telling him that he got you hot." Shorty showed Mike the text exchange. "We're gonna figure this out without Mitch. I just want you to know that I didn't know it was gonna happen like this."

Mike looked Shorty in the eye and knew he was telling the truth. It was a huge weight off his shoulders.

The next day, Mike was relieved to wake up with a clear head. It was time to think of a new plan. Honey was the only person he could trust and after their breakup, he didn't know what to do. There were times he thought about reconciliation, but so much damage had been done he didn't think he could ever trust her again. He knew he had to man up and not depend on anyone else to fix his mistakes and bad decisions. Ultimately, it was his own responsibility to straighten out his life and no one else's. Not Honey's, not the lawyers', not his parents, not Shorty. It was Mike and Mike alone. It was time to own everything.

He still had some money left over from the house that he sold, and he wanted to invest his money into a property. He went on the internet looking for foreclosures and short sales. He knew that the market was in an upswing. Everything he saw was either too expensive or needed too much work. A lot of the properties were in Queens and the Bronx, neither of which he was interested in. Weeks went by and nothing good came along. Mike called his mom to talk to her about his status and what had been going on in his life lately. He was getting hopeless and there were times where he even thought about turning himself in. He didn't even care anymore. It was hard to do all this alone. His resolve was weakening. He was still damaged from the breakup with Honey. He had a better life with Honey and Myah in Florida, and he missed that. Mike didn't like New York anymore. It was a place that only brought bad memories. It was his past, and it was not working as his present. It was nothing but a graveyard of memories and bad decisions. New York saw his future as small, petty. The city didn't care, so why should Mike?

His mom could see he was very depressed and suggested he turn himself in. She suggested an Asian lawyer, as she thought that they might care a little more. He wanted to handle it on his own, not with anyone else's advice. He went back to looking for properties. He focused on Staten Island. The houses were cheaper there, and he was trying to make the best investment possible before he ran out of money. He knew what he had left wouldn't last long. After weeks of looking, he found a handyman special. It definitely needed some work, but the price made it desirable. He put in an offer, and they countered it after a few days of negotiations. The price seemed right.

He had to tell Honey and Myah he would be moving soon. He knew that Myah would be hurt, but he needed a serious change in life. He felt like there was more of a risk of getting caught if he was living in Queens. He called Honey to tell her he was moving to Staten Island and that he could only see Myah on weekends. She didn't care much. They barely spoke as it was and, when they did, it was all about Myah. Myah was upset because she was getting used to seeing her dad again and didn't want him to move so far away. He tried to explain to her that he was buying a house with a backyard and a driveway and a lot more space. She cried, but he comforted her by telling her they would soon have a house again. They both laughed and Mike asked: "Why did I move back to New York, Myah?"

"For me," she said.

"So, if I moved back to New York all the way from Florida for you, Staten Island is easy breezy." They laughed and hugged. "I want to move to Staten Island with Daddy." Mike knew this would not be possible. Now was not the time.

He wanted to close on the property as soon as possible. The house was under his parents' names. The only people he could trust now were his immediate family. His parents had some debt to clear before they could officially close on the house. Mike ended up clearing the debt for them so that the closing would go smoothly.

It was getting closer to the closing date, and he had to drive to Staten Island for the last inspection of the house. This would also be a good time for Mike to check out his neighbors. He got there an hour early so he could drive around and check out the area. The neighborhood was diverse with a good mix of people. Being in a neighborhood with a predominant race would make Mike stick out. Even in a neighborhood with Asians, Mike stood out. He had *always* stood out, no matter where he was. He had a distinct demeanor that made him shine.

The realtor finally came. The closing was all set for next week. Mike noticed some minor things that needed fixing, but everything looked good to him for the most part. He drove back to Queens to pack. While he was packing, a neighbor knocked on the door. He felt nervous and paranoid because his neighbors had never knocked on his door before. With everything happening he felt more conspicuous and vulnerable than usual. He answered the door with a smile on his face.

"How can I help you?"

"Someone came to my house and gave me their phone number and asked for you to call them."

"Who?" Mike was shocked and bugged the fuck out.

"The person said that he knocked on your door, but no one answered. I was outside cleaning my porch and he handed me his number and asked me to give it to you." Mike didn't know what to do. He went to his car and called the number.

"Hello. You gave your number to my neighbor for me to get in touch with you?"

"I don't want to disturb you, but I am the neighbor's

son. You spoke to my parents outside of the house in Staten Island.

"How do you know where I live?"

"I followed you."

"Followed me? What the fuck you following me for? Are you some type of fucking weirdo? I'm gonna call the cops!"

"I just want to say I don't think that you should buy that house."

"What? Why not?" Mike knew his neighbor was blockbusting.

"The house needs a lot of work and I thought you might want to know."

"I'm good, thanks," Mike said and hung up the phone. Now he knew his neighbors were nosy. He still thought that it was kind of awkward that this guy followed him home to tell him about the house. He had already invested so much time and money into the house. If he backed out now, he would have to start over.

Closing day came, and Mike went to Staten Island with his parents to finish the deal. His parents signed the necessary documents and Mike got the keys to his new house. After the closing, they all went to the new house. Mike took notes of repairs and things that needed to be done. He was going to live on the first floor and rent out the second floor, which would help pay his mortgage. He was still living in Queens but needed to fix the first floor of the new house so he could move in as soon as possible. He was paying rent and a mortgage now. He had less than $100,000 in savings and no secondary income. Everything had to be on a tight budget.

The renovation was going to take about a month and would cost $40,000. Once the house was renovated, he had a tenant within a few weeks. Everything was going smoothly. He was picking Myah up every weekend and spending quality time with her. He felt like everything was slowly starting to come together, but his legal situation still hung over his head.

His tenant was paying 85% of the mortgage. Mike started to look for a new lawyer. He wanted to find the best criminal defense attorney in Brooklyn. After searching for a few hours, he found an attorney named Julie, whom he had heard about before, and called her. He briefly explained his case and they agreed to meet in the next week.

She was expensive. Her retainer was $10,000, which was out of Mike's price range. He was suspicious of her and thought she might be setting him up like his other lawyers.

Once inside, he told Julie his story. He told her how his previous lawyers had done him wrong and how Mitch had the cops come to his house. He didn't want to hire someone that was going to do the same thing. Julie was surprised by Mike's story and said she wasn't worried about the case because he never pleaded guilty. She was concerned about the parole violation.

"You're going to owe them time. I just want you to be aware of the situation. We can try to work out a deal from the outside, but I'm going to have to make some phone calls tomorrow. How quickly do you want to take care of this?"

"Probably after Christmas. I would like to spend Christmas with my daughter."

He left the office feeling good and feeling relieved. For a brief moment he even allowed himself to feel a tiny bit of hope, something he had not felt in an awfully long time. He sent Honey a text letting her know what was going on and that she might need to take care of Myah for a little while longer. There was still the chance that he would have to do some time for the parole violation. Honey still hadn't responded to his text. An hour later she replied: "Ok." She asked Mike if he could start picking Myah up. She had had Lasik surgery and wouldn't be able to drive for a few weeks. Mike noticed Honey was calmer than usual. He wondered if she was over the breakup, over him. She was good at keeping her feelings to herself. He made it a point to keep their conversations short. He was still hurting from the breakup and their conversations, once they spread beyond the scope of taking care of Myah, could get very ugly.

Thursday came around and Mike had to meet with Shorty Roc. Shorty gave Mike a stack to put down for his lawyer's fee. Mike had told Shorty about Julie's high fee and Shorty offered to pay it. They met at Mike's new crib and smoked and chilled for a minute. Shorty handed Mike a thousand dollars, all in $10 bills.

Mike took the train to Julie's office. He was excited and hoped to hear some good news.

"So, how's everything? I got your paperwork, and it looks like what they did was totally illegal. It seems you were a victim of entrapment."

"Yes, I was set up."

"I wish you had hired me from the beginning. I could have beaten this or got you time served. I don't think they'll let you walk out of court the same day. I do see them dropping the charges or giving you time served, though. The only problem is parole. They might want you to do the remaining time incarcerated. Are you willing to do the 17 months?"

"I am, but I already know that's a worst-case-scenario. I'm hiring you to get the least amount of time possible."

"I'm just being honest. We are going to fight, but I want you to know it's going to be difficult. Be prepared to do a few months. Would you be willing to do a year if it came down to that?"

"No. I haven't been running this long to do a year. They are trying to punish me for something that happened 10 years ago. What they did was totally illegal. I'm not the same person that I was 10 years ago."

"It helps that you haven't gotten into any trouble. If we can prove you are not hiding, it will be good for your case. Let's talk after Christmas."

II

This was Mike's first Christmas in his new house and he wanted to invite his family to celebrate with him. He was in good spirits and felt that things were looking better. He was seeing Myah every weekend and he and Honey hadn't argued in a while. He went all out and bought everyone gifts, he decorated the house, got a huge tree. Myah was going to have a good Christmas. He wasn't sure when he would turn himself in. All he wanted was to make every day a good experience. His freedom could be taken away at any moment, and he wanted to make the most out of his time.

Honey texted Mike and asked if Myah could stay with him for most of her winter recess. She was busy with work and thought Mike would like to spend as much time with her while he could. They agreed on a schedule that had Mike feeling optimistic.

Mike was preparing to do a short bid and knew that every minute with Myah was important. He wrapped seven presents for Myah, as this was her seventh Christmas. He knew she wasn't happy he lived in Staten Island. They only saw each other on the weekends, so he wanted to make Christmas special for her. Picking Myah up was always the best part of his week. This was the first time he would have her for more than a week. He was excited.

When he got to Honey's house, her father came downstairs. He had a weird look on his face and slammed the door after Mike put Myah in the car. Mike wondered what was up with all the tension.

Myah fell asleep on the ride. Mike woke her up to see the house lit up with Christmas decorations. She was ecstatic. Myah ran to the door. The moment she walked in her eyes lit up.

"Is this for us?" Myah asked.

"No, it's for you. I got my Christmas gift already."

"What is it?"

"You, silly. We can't open anything until Christmas."

"Oh c'mon! Please, just one?"

"No, Myah. You have to wait until Christmas." Of course, he gave in let her open one of her gifts. She chose one of the bigger gifts, which was a doll house. He told her it was like the one they had in Florida. It made her sad.

"Daddy, I love you. Just give me a hug."

"What's wrong? Does this give you bad memories?"

"No, just good memories of mommy and daddy together."

"Myah, everything will be okay."

She broke down.

"Why are you crying?" Mike wiped the tears from her cheeks.

"I wish you and mommy would just say sorry."

"Myah, I didn't break up with mommy and it's too late to say sorry. It doesn't work like that."

Myah looked at her dad, frustrated. "This is the worst day ever!"

"Do you want to go back to mommy's house?" She nodded. "Myah, you're acting spoiled."

Mike texted Honey. "Myah is upset about us again."

Honey called and spoke to Myah. Mike couldn't hear the entire conversation, but he heard Myah say yes. She apologized to Mike and gave him a hug. He knew it wasn't her fault. She was just venting. He held her close, and they fell asleep together.

The next morning Honey sent a few pictures of some presents for Myah. In one of the pictures Mike noticed a wheelchair in the background. He didn't say anything to Honey. He said that Myah would love the gifts and Honey asked if she was still awake. The moment Mike said yes, Honey called to wish Myah a Merry Christmas. Myah was so happy to hear her voice.

Mike couldn't help but wonder if everything was okay with Honey. She hadn't been texting much lately and seemed more distant than usual. On Christmas day, Mike texted her and said he hoped she felt better. Honey texted back and said that she'd just been very tired lately and that the medication was taking a toll on her. He sent her some pictures of Myah having a good time. They built a snowman and had snowball fights. He bought a sled and pulled her through the park. They had a few great days together. On the 29th, Mike had a talk with her and asked if she would ever want to move to Staten Island.

"Mommy needs me, Daddy. Maybe next year."

"I need you, too, Myah. You make me so happy." She made a sad face.

"I'm sorry, Daddy."

"What do you mean? Why are you sorry?"

"I'm sorry that I picked mommy in Florida, and we left you." Mike's eyes welled up with tears and he started to cry.

"Myah, nothing is your fault. Mommy and I grew apart. That has nothing to do with you. We both love you very much."

The next day he took her home. He wanted to see

Honey. He felt he should check on her. He was about five minutes away when she texted him: *I'm not home but my brother is waiting there for Myah.*

Mike had never been on good terms with Honey's brother, Dee. They usually didn't even speak to one another. He dropped Myah off and left. He still couldn't shake the feeling that something was off. She wasn't acting like herself. She was avoiding him; it had been a month since he last saw her.

Is everything ok with you? Mike texted. No answer. He texted her again. When she didn't answer again, he called her. She didn't answer, and, instead, replied with a text; *I'll call you back in a minute.* He answered on the first ring.

"Hey, is everything ok?"

"Everything is ok with Myah, but I'm a little fucked up. I can barely walk."

"What? What do you mean fucked up? What do you mean you can barely walk?"

"They found a cyst in my brain."

There was silence.

It was momentary, but it was deep. Mike's thoughts whirled and he felt physically ill. He couldn't believe what he just heard. "Wait, what? A cyst? Are you okay? What the fuck, why didn't you tell me earlier?"

"I didn't want to worry you and I didn't think

you cared about me anymore." Mike was in shock and breathing heavily. "Why is this happening to you? Why didn't you tell me earlier? How can I turn myself in now? I can't. Who's gonna take care of Myah? Who's gonna take care of you?"

"Mike, take care of what you gotta do. We will be alright. My parents are here with me, and they will help with Myah."

"No way am I going to accept a year now. How can I? I would go crazy in there knowing you are sick. You helped me so much, let me help you now. I'm gonna sell this house and move back to Queens so that I can be closer to you guys."

"That would be great. Myah will be so happy."

Chapter 11: Nothing is Promised

I

Mike was in complete shock. Why her? Did the breakup have something to do with it? Was it the Lasik? Maybe the way she ate? Honey was skinny but she ate everything. He couldn't think straight. He had to focus on what he was going to do next. He got a piece of paper and wrote down his short-term goals in order of importance.

Number one was to sell the house. Then, he needed to talk to his lawyer and tell her he couldn't do too much time. He needed to be there for Honey and Myah.

Mike called a realtor and put the house on the market that same week. He told the tenant he was selling the house. She was not happy. She demanded Mike pay her to move. Mike was under so much stress that he blew up on her and they argued. The cops came. It went on and on, but finally, after weeks of arguing, he made peace with the tenant.

The diagnosis was worse than Mike could have imagined. Brain cancer. She was fucking 33 years old. This couldn't possibly be real. How could this be real? He went to see her. He was shocked by her appearance. She looked frail. Diminished.

"Honey, why did you wait so long to tell me?"

"I didn't know how to tell you. I didn't think you cared." Mike was stunned. He felt like he had been kicked.

"Didn't care? Honey, I love you more than anyone in the entire world, how could I not care. You are the mother of my daughter. No matter what, you will always be in my heart. Of course I care," he said tenderly, wiping away the tears from her face. "We've been through so much. This is just another obstacle we will have to overcome."

"Mike, I am paralyzed from the waist down."

He was devastated. He had had no idea just how bad

it was.

"I'm losing my memory," she continued. "Everything hurts. It even hurts when I chew."

It was then that the full force of this hit him. He was watching the person he loved slowly die right in front of him.

II

Mike's brain was in overdrive. He couldn't help Honey, no one could. So, he concentrated only on the practical things that lay before him. Things that he could control. He started with his case. He had to speak to Julie. There was no way he could do any time right now, not with Honey's situation and Myah needing her father. Just thinking of Myah made him begin to crumble, but he fought to keep it together. He wanted Julie to use Honey's illness to milk every bit of sympathy that he could. Fuck it, he thought. The ends would justify the means. He was willing to do anything to stay out of jail and to be there for Myah.

He texted Honey every day to check up on her. He felt like he owed her, and he would do whatever it took to be there for her. His emotions were tied up in an extraordinarily complex and complicated knot when it came to Honey. There was fear and sadness, of course, but underneath were blacker feelings. He was angry and he didn't understand why. He was overcome with huge, racking waves of guilt over being angry. He was confused by his anger. Could he possibly be mad at Honey? That didn't make any sense. He searched his heart deeply and found no malice towards Honey. Even at their most vitriolic, even during their most vicious and volatile fights, Mike never felt a hatred towards Honey. So, was he angry at the cancer itself? That didn't make any sense. He was angry at his inability to save her.

When Mike had been in need, she had dropped everything, rearranged her entire life, and fled the state with him. That's something that went beyond love. To Mike, her sacrifices bordered on the holy. And now he was helpless to do anything that would save her. He couldn't repay the debt he owed her, and it killed him.

She was heroic in her acceptance of this sentence and saintly in her quiet struggle. She amazed Mike with her strength and dignity. He was constantly apologizing to her for not being a better person, father, and husband. She admonished him for his unnecessary and profuse apologies. It was just the way life was, she would say. It was no one's fault, least of all his. That did little to comfort him. She was more worried about him than she was for herself.

"You're stronger than me, Honey. You can beat this."

"We are gonna beat this. We just need to protect Myah. She still doesn't know that you know yet," She was struggling to talk. It was barely noticeable to everyone but Mike, but he saw it. He saw it and he felt it.

"You don't need to worry about any of those things right now. All you need to do is focus on getting better. If you need anything at all, any day, any time, I'm always here for you."

III

Mike was losing track of the days. Everything seemed to run together. He was terrified he would eventually forget Honey; what she looked like, the sound of her voice, the little things that never seemed to mean anything until now. Now they were *everything*.

Mike had an appointment with his lawyer. He told her about Honey's diagnosis, and she seemed genuinely concerned. He wanted to know if this new development could have any bearing on his case. He stressed over and over to Julie how important it was for him to get the quickest sentence possible. She asked him to produce proof of Honey's diagnosis. Initially he was annoyed and felt like she didn't believe him, but she explained they would need to present evidence to a judge. He texted Honey and asked her to email her medical records to Julie.

The next day, he met up with Shorty Roc to vent. Mike was very emotional. Shorty offered to take him for a night out. They went to a club called Vodka in Washington Heights. Shorty was treated like a don everywhere he went. Free bottles, girls shaking their asses everywhere, it was lit. Mike wanted to get drunk to escape, even if it was just for the night. He had never been under so much pressure before. He just kept telling himself things would get better. He needed to focus on taking care of his warrant. He needed to fix the problems with his tenant. Honey was fighting for her life, and everything was closing in on him. It was suffocating.

His funds were dwindling, so he decided to sell his car. He also had some more jewelry he could pawn. He looked for an affordable car. He found one that was pretty decent. He got $10,000 for his old car and paid six months of payments for the new car up front. Once he sold his house, he would use those funds to get a nicer car. He would get his jewelry out of the pawn shop, and everything would even out.

The next day, Mike went to Julie's office and didn't bring any money. He wanted to hear what she had to say. He felt like she was avoiding him.

"Did you talk to the district attorney?"

"Yes, I did. They are willing to offer a year. What do you think?"

"A year? Maybe I would have taken that before, but not now."

He had been railroaded from the very beginning and his past was being used against him. "I was scared then," Mike explained. "I'm not scared now." It wasn't just talk; it was true. For years he had been terrified of the system. The cops, the D.A.s, the judges, the bullshit. He had lived in constant fear of being caught and going back to prison. Honey had been right all those years ago – he *was* selfish. Well, not anymore. After seeing Honey's struggle, he feared *nothing* now.

"This is just their first offer. Let me work with the District Attorney. I have a good relationship with him. He owes me a favor. Maybe I can have him do something," Julie said.

Mike got up to leave when Julie asked if he had payment.

"Not today. I had to take care of some bills."

The next day, Mike called Julie again and it went straight to voicemail. There wasn't even any point in continuing to call her since he couldn't accept the deal being offered right now. He needed to behave more strategically.

Mike called the realtor to see what was happening with the prospective buyers. He was working on a mortgage commitment.

Mike still had to talk with Myah about everything. Before he picked her up, he wrote down some thoughts. He texted Honey when he got there, and she told him to come in and that her parents had left. There was still some tension there, so Mike was happy to avoid them. He walked upstairs and saw Honey on the couch, sitting upright. Mike looked at her and immediately broke down.

"Mike, you need to keep it together, please. Myah is in her room. I told her that I wanted to talk to you first." Myah came running as soon as she heard Mike's voice. "Daddy!" She screamed, running to hug him. "It's ok, Daddy. Mommy said she's getting better," Myah said, wiping away her dad's tears.

"Myah, get your things ready and be on good behavior with your dad."

"Do you need anything? " Mike asked, wiping more tears away, trying to compose himself.

"You're helping so much by taking care of Myah and being such a great dad." Mike couldn't believe Honey was complimenting him. She hadn't done that since they broke up.

"Are you sure you're ok? Do you need anything before I leave?"

"Just a bottle of water," Honey said, looking down. She couldn't bear to look at Mike and started to cry. He hugged her close.

"You're gonna get better and I'm here for you, always."

"Thank you so much. I think you should go before my parents see you."

Mike didn't want to leave.

"Please," she asked, wiping away tears. "This is too much for me."

He didn't want to stress her out, so he hugged and kissed her. "Myah, you ready?"

"Let's go, Daddy." She gave her mom a hug and a kiss goodbye. "I'll see you Sunday, mommy."

"Be a good girl for your dad."

Mike felt like they were a family again, and it had been a long time since he had felt that way. He drove Myah back to Staten Island. He hated being so far away from Honey and Myah during this time. As soon as he got to the house, he called the realtor.

"Congratulations!" the realtor said. "They just signed the contract! We need to get your parents' signatures and we'll be ready to roll."

"How long until we close?"

"It should be about 60 days, give or take."

It was going to be a long 60 days, but good things

were in motion. Mike called his parents to tell them the news. They were happy, proud, and relieved.

"Mom, none of this feels real. Why Honey? Why is this happening to her? She's the most considerate person I know. She taught me to think of others first," Mike told his mom through tears.

"I know it's not fair. Honey is like my daughter." They both cried in silence for a few moments.

"Mom, no one has helped me as much as Honey and you and dad. I would seriously do anything for you all." He felt a deep, sweeping wave of gratitude come over him like a breaking dawn. A measure of humility came with it. All these people, his family, his closest friends, had all stepped up in some way to help him through his years on the run. He had never truly known the meaning of gratitude until that moment. He felt like he owed them all so much and he'd never be able to properly repay them. That, more than anything, had been what made him able to survive those hard years in strange places, those long nights locked down in incarceration. That had been his strength and his soul, whether he had known it consciously or not at the time.

IV

Over the next few days, Mike stayed focused on the house. He had to get an appraisal, but the tenant was still giving him a hard time. She kept making excuses for not being home. He didn't want beef with her. She hadn't paid rent in months. The buyers were becoming increasingly frustrated and told him that if they couldn't go upstairs, they didn't want the house. She was playing petty games, trying to get a rise out of him. She was trying to get him locked up so she could live in the house rent-free. Mike had bigger problems. He offered to pay her a month's rent if she moved. She agreed and Mike was able to set an appointment for the appraisers to look at the entire house. When he texted the realtor, he was told the buyers had changed their minds.

Mike was frustrated. He had wasted an entire month and now there was no end in sight. This felt like the biggest test of his life. He felt like a failure. He felt like he had failed the only person that had helped him. He apologized to Honey, and she told him not to worry.

The house re-listed at a reduced price. Mike got a few offers, but nothing worth entertaining. He was desperate, but the house was already below market value.

He didn't want to short himself. He spoke to Honey about doing something for Myah on her birthday.

"You can have her all week, I just want her here on her actual birthday," she said.

"Maybe we should all do something together. It would make Myah happy to see us together." She was quiet. Mike heard her sniffling. "Honey, please don't cry."

"Maybe next year when I get better. I don't want to be there in a wheelchair."

"Sometimes I seriously can't believe this is happening."

"It's life," Honey said softly.

Mike was deeply affected by everything that was going on. He told himself he had to be strong and give Myah a good birthday. He was going to surprise her when he picked her up next week. He knew that she would be so happy and surprised to see the house decorated for her. Mike didn't know where his strength would come from, and he was afraid that each test would be the last one.

He kept trying to get in touch with his lawyer but had no luck. He didn't even bother leaving messages. He heard back from the realtor. There was an offer on the house. It was lower than what Mike had been hoping for. In the end, he accepted.

From Monday through Thursday, Mike would sell the things he wasn't taking with him. On Fridays, he would pick up Myah and drop her back off on Sunday. Structure was something Mike learned while in prison, and he had really applied that lesson while they were all living in Florida. He needed to get back to that, especially for Myah's sake. His experiences had taught him ways to survive.

He was running low on funds and starting to worry. He had barely $1,500 left. The sale was taking a long time to go through; it would be months before everything was secure and processed. The buyers had run into a problem getting a mortgage. Mike decided to call Shorty Roc and ask him for a small loan of $2,000. Shorty gave him $1,000 and told him that if he dropped a package off for him, he would give Mike another rack. Mike agreed without even asking. He didn't need to. He was desperate and he needed the money.

Shorty gave him an address and a small duffle bag. Mike went to the address. A hot Latina girl came out, took the bag, smiled at Mike, and left. After the drop, he went back to Shorty Roc's crib. Shorty gave him an extra $500 and laughed as he told Mike he had just paid him to deliver clothes to Shorty's ex. It had been a test, and Mike had passed. Every friendship has a base, and their friendship was based on straight up loyalty.

Mike had enough money to hold him down until he closed on the house now. He was relieved and felt like he could breathe for a bit. Then he got a text from the tenant accusing him of turning the air conditioning off. Mike had no idea what she was talking about, so he called a local HVAC company. The repairman was there within the hour. The unit was shot, and it was going to cost $2,000 to repair. He wanted to avoid problems with the tenant at all costs, so he knew he needed to take care of this as soon as possible. He wanted this nightmare tenant out immediately. He had to think of something to keep him going until he closed on the house. He called a few friends up to see if they knew of any jobs that paid in cash. His friend Joe was managing a car dealership and offered him a job, but it was in the Bronx. Mike was desperate so he accepted it. He worked ten hours a day, and it took him 3 hours to commute. It took time away from him, away from his family. He spent his one day off with Myah. It hurt him to not be able to provide for his family, but he didn't want to burden Honey with his problems.

Mike had been working for about a month, and he felt distant from Myah and Honey because the job was taking up so much of his time. He couldn't wait to close on his house so he could quit. He got a call from the realtor telling him the buyers wouldn't be able to close the following month.

V

Honey told Mike she was on some new medication and wouldn't be able to text as much. He asked if she was ok, and she said that she was. He asked if there was anything that he could do to help. She asked him to bring her a blunt. Mike expressed concerns about her smoking while she was sick, but he couldn't say no to her. He rolled up two joints, put them in a bag, and gave them to her. The next day, he went to pick up Myah. Honey's father brought her downstairs. Mike gave him the shopping bag and told him it was for Honey.

In the car, Mike asked Myah how Honey had been doing. Myah said she had just been sleeping a lot. Mike just said, "ok." He didn't want to put any pressure on Myah, even though he was desperate for details on Honey's day-to-day condition. He knew she couldn't comprehend the situation. It was hard for Mike to digest everything, but he knew he had to be strong for everyone. "Don't worry, Myah. mommy will get better soon, and everything will be back to normal."

He texted Honey every day. Sometimes she would respond, sometimes she wouldn't. Most of the time, when she did respond, her text messages didn't make sense.

The realtor called. He had a closing date, and it was only three weeks away. He had been able to get rid of his nightmare tenant after much hassling back and forth. It had been painful, but she was finally out, and Mike could move forward. He found an apartment ten minutes from Honey's house. He would be closer to them, and he would have money. Everything looked promising again, and he had what he wanted: he was close to his family.

VI

Mike was at work when his phone started ringing and he saw that it was Honey's brother, Dee, calling. Mike was concerned. It was unusual for Honey's brother to call him.

"Mike, where are you right now?"

"I'm at work. Is everything ok with Myah and Honey?"

"Myah is ok, but are you by yourself?"

Mike stepped outside. "Now I am, what's up?"

"Honey's cancer is terminal."

Mike lost it. "What do you mean?" He was yelling.

"I know you're upset but you need to calm down. If you're gonna act erratic maybe you shouldn't come."

"Where is she? Dee, tell me right now."

"We are at Flushing Hospital."

"I'll be right there."

Mike told his boss that he was leaving immediately and needed to get paid. His boss told him to come back the following week. Joe saw the look on Mike's face and intervened. Mike waited a long five minutes. Joe came out with $800. Mike grabbed it and ran.

He was speeding, cutting cars off, trying to get to the hospital. He had to see Honey immediately. He couldn't believe that this was happening. He was punching the steering wheel as hard as he could. His parents called him crying.

Mike saw Honey laying in the bed. She could barely open her eyes. It was worse than he had imagined. He saw his best friend on her deathbed.

"I'm here, Honey. I'm gonna stay with you."

Honey didn't reply. She just nodded her head.

"We've been through so much. You can beat this. You're the strongest person I know. Please, Myah and I need you. How are we gonna survive? We were supposed to do this together. You can't leave me," Mike was pleading through his tears. So many emotions were going through him. He could not bear to see her like that, to see her so weak and timid, almost like she wasn't fully there. She looked so small. It felt like he was watching her disappear in real time. The light that once surrounded her entire being was dimming.

He went outside to get some air and to wait for his sister. Amy pulled up and the moment she saw Mike her heart broke for him. They talked for a few minutes. They got themselves together enough to go inside. They sat there waiting for their turn to see Honey. Only four people were allowed up at a time. Honey's parents were upstairs with her. Mike saw Dee talking to one of the doctors.

"What's going on? Can we do something about this? Is there any possible way? It can't be over."

"I'm so sorry. We tried everything. She has another cyst in an area that we aren't able to reach."

"You have to be kidding. There has to be something that you can do. You *have* to help her."

"They tried everything, Mike," Dee said quietly.

"I have to go back upstairs to see her."

"It might be better if you go home for a little bit and come back tomorrow."

"I'm not going anywhere," Mike said, crying and angry.

"You have to be strong for Myah, Mike. Honey would want that." Dee said. He was beginning to talk like she was already gone. It was not lost on Mike, but he pushed it out of his mind.

"Where's Myah right now?"

"She's still in school. You should go home and

prepare for the worst," Dee said.

Mike didn't say anything. He just sat there and looked around. Everyone was looking at him. He could not stop crying. His face was hot and flushed. He had to get out. He didn't say any goodbyes. He just walked to his car and left. He went home and wrote down what he had to do. His entire life had just been cataclysmically upended. Now his plan was to make sure that he would always protect his daughter from what was going on.

He called Dee first thing the next day. "How is she?"

"Not good. She's going to be admitted to a hospice today."

"No, that's where they go to die. Don't do anything until I get there."

"It's not your decision to make, Mike. As her caretaker and brother, I know what is best for her right now," Dee said.

Mike didn't want to fight. It was not the time for that. "What is the address of the hospice?"

"I can hear it in your voice, you're stressed. You need to stay home today. It's not good for Honey."

"Please give me the address." Mike was getting desperate, but he knew he had to hold it together.

"Come tomorrow."

"Okay," Mike said, feeling defeated. He didn't want to make things worse. Honey's parents were losing their daughter. Dee was losing his sister, and Mike was losing his best friend, his daughter's mother, his support system. She was everything to Mike. More than just a girlfriend, more than just his baby's mother. For years he had called her his "wife." Though they hadn't officially married, she would always be his wife.

Mike went out drinking. He couldn't stay home alone. It drove him crazy. He had to be around people. He went home after two drinks.

The next morning, as Mike was getting ready to see Honey, he called Dee. There was no answer. As he was putting his sneakers on and about to leave, Dee called him back.

"Hey Mike, are you alone?"

"Yeah, what's going on?"

"Mike... Honey just passed away."

Mike hung up the phone and sat utterly motionless. That was it. She was gone. Just like that.

Everything stopped and all he heard was the dull, useless thud of his heartbeat in his ears. It all fell away. Everything. It all went black. Every bit of breath was sucked from Mike's body. He didn't care. Even the simple act of breathing seemed meaningless. He let the blackness engulf him and he slumped down into it like comfort.

After a while, he found himself watching old videos on his phone, just to hear Honey's voice and see her face. He hadn't even realized he was doing it; he had no conscious memory of looking for the videos or starting them up. Everything was hazy. He was currently watching footage from when they lived in Florida. To see Honey walking and happy was devastating. He just wanted her back. He felt anger and frustration. He called Dee back.

"Dee. I need to come to the hospice right now."

"My entire family is here. I don't think it's a good time for you to come."

"Okay, but where is Myah?"

"She's here, too, Mike."

"What? Listen, I don't want Myah there. I don't want her to be traumatized."

Dee disagreed. "It's good for her to see her mom. This is her last time."

Mike was furious. He hung up the phone. He had been the closest person to Honey for years. *How the fuck are they going to exclude me?* Mike thought to himself.

After a while, Dee called Mike back and Myah was on the phone.

"Daddy, Mommy is in heaven now and she is not in any more pain."

"How are you, Myah? Do you want me to pick you up?"

"No, I want to stay here tonight."

"Are you sure?"

"Yes."

He didn't want to pressure her. He told her he would see soon.

"Okay, Daddy. I love you."

After Myah hung up, Mike texted Shorty Roc to tell him what happened. Shorty told him to come over. He drove to Shorty Roc's in a heavy silence. It felt like nothing mattered. He was just focused on not being alone.

VII

The next day, Mike had to buy a suit. The service was in a few days and Honey's parents wanted the wake and funeral to be done as soon as possible. They were grief-stricken and distraught. Mike couldn't believe that he was buying a suit for Honey's funeral. Everything was unreal. The last time Mike went to buy a suit was when they went searching for Honey's wedding dress. Mike's pain was unbearable, but he had to be stronger than ever. That week, he was going to Honey's service. The following week, he was closing on his house and moving to Queens. The real-time details of everyday life were not going to wait just because Mike had suffered this loss. In some instinctual way he knew it was good for him to keep busy. At every quiet, reflective interval he would mourn. He had never been through anything like this. Every time he felt weak, he had to remind himself of how strongly she had believed in him. No one would ever understand. He felt like he couldn't talk to anyone. Mike was imprisoned within his grief. He didn't know what was ahead of him, but he knew that Myah was going to need him more than ever.

Mike's plans had changed. He couldn't turn himself in now. Depending on lawyers to give him his life back didn't seem realistic anymore. The pressure he was under would have broken him 10, 15 years ago, but not now. He tried not thinking about Honey. He tried to focus on the next two weeks, but it was difficult. Just thinking about the funeral had him shook in a way he had never known.

He was in the darkest place he had ever known. He felt violent. He wanted to hurt someone badly. He wanted the world to feel the pain and anger he felt.

Mike was no stranger to death. The violent world of his youth had taught him many things about death and dying, suffering. He had seen friends die right in front of him. It had hardened him, but this was different. This was so much worse.

He looked for ways to vent out his anger. He couldn't see a psychiatrist, that just wasn't his thing. He couldn't talk to a stranger, and he knew he couldn't trust a doctor. He went to the gym three times a day trying to distract himself with intense physical activity. He tried to tire himself out just so he could get some sleep. None of it work. Every time he slowed down for even a second the intrusive thoughts and images would torture him. He was becoming the darkness inside of him, and he knew he was losing himself in it. Part of him did not mind the idea of becoming completely lost, of finally surrendering and letting it all go, drowning in it.

And then, with whiplash speed and force, he would snap back into himself, anchored by one purpose: Myah.

Mike remembered all the things he learned from Honey. He remembered all the things this American culture he was a part of had taught him. It had taken him most of his life to sort through all this chaos; to separate information from emotion and to truly learn and advance from the wisdom he had gained, through failure and success, through joy and despair, to his life going forward.

The most important thing Mike had learned, though was this: it wasn't about him.

It never was.

He understood it now. This life wasn't for him or about him. Life was for his child.

Life was for the people he loved, not himself. It only became meaningful when he let himself go and lived solely and purposefully for Myah. Honey had tried to teach him this, but he was too young, too stupid. He wasn't ready.

Now he was.

VIII

Weeks went by and Mike was playing out his days in a haze of grief. He couldn't concentrate. The funeral had come and gone like a dream, and he had trouble remembering any of it.

He had established a simple routine that allowed him to emotionally subsist, but that was about it. He was picking up Myah on Fridays to spend the weekend, then he would drop her off at school on Monday. He couldn't remember what he was doing during the rest of the week. Very little, if that.

He knew he couldn't be a weekend dad anymore. He knew what needed to be done. He had to take on both roles in her life. Mike quit his job to spend more time with Myah. He found an apartment 10 minutes away from her grandparents' house. On his way to tell her, he found himself smiling, happy that he was moving, happy to be putting a plan, any kind of plan, into motion. Myah was ecstatic to have him so close.

Slow, small steps was his mantra. He began fixing up the new place for Myah so she would feel like it was her home.

Mike had also been considering opening business.

He liked the idea of being his own boss. He also did something very out of character: he joined social media.

Things were going smoothly until one day Mike got a phone call from a private number. Normally he wouldn't answer a number he didn't know, but something made him take the call. It was Shorty Roc's friend, GS, calling on behalf of Shorty. Mike knew immediately something wasn't right. When GS explained Shorty was locked up (and not dead, as Mike had feared), he was relieved. Shocked, but relieved.

GS didn't want to get into specifics over the phone, so they agreed to meet in person. They smoked a blunt and GS started telling Mike what happened to Shorty.

"They're charging him with trafficking." Mike knew the drill.

He gave GS a hundred for Shorty's account. He knew it would be dangerous for him if he kept too close to Shorty's situation, so he agreed to speak to Shorty through GS.

Mike was thinking about how anyone can get caught lacking out there. Shorty was a smart dude but all it takes is one mistake and your life can be over. Mike wanted to turn himself in because he wanted everything behind him. He didn't know how to do it without traumatizing Myah. He had to beat the case. It was the only way.

He had to distance himself from his old life and

from the streets. He dreamed of being a boss, his own boss, doing something he enjoyed. Anything. He was ready to be done with the stress. He was ready to be done with all of it.

He thought of all the people who had come and gone in his life. He saw the faces of the friends he'd lost to prison or violence. He saw the faces of the people he'd hurt, the victims he'd terrorized. He flashed on all the memories of the harm and fear he'd created for others. He let those memories pummel him with guilt and he forced himself to see the faces of his victims.

He found himself wondering what life would have been like had he been born elsewhere, something he seemed to be doing more often lately. What if he had never been introduced to the streets, what would he have become? What if he had had the opportunity to go to college? Where would he be right now? It was a fool's errand, but it was something his idle thoughts couldn't resist. It was a strange life.

IX

It was getting colder. The change of seasons always affected Mike in strange ways. The air smelled like Halloween. It made him feel like a kid.

He had spent a lot of solitary time thinking hard on his next moves. Every instinct told him to keep running, that he could beat this, but part of him was resisting this idea. It was like another voice in his head, a deeper, more deliberate voice, telling him that running was a child's game and it was time for him to be a man. He didn't know this voice and didn't recognize it at all, even though it was his own. The voice was right. It was time to end this.

Turning himself wasn't going to be easy, but he knew he had to dig deep down and find the strength and the resolve to see it through. He had to narrow his focus down to one goal: Myah.

His fear preyed on the blackness of not knowing what was going to happen. To surrender himself meant giving up all control over his life and that was such a difficult thing for him to even think about, let alone perform.

He didn't know what was going to happen. It could be a few days, a few weeks a few months… It could end up being a year and a half. He knew he had a year and a half left on his parole from his previous bid. He knew if he got some hotshot D.A., some overzealous politician trying to make a name for himself, it could go very badly.

Mike wanted to spend Christmas and New Year's with his family. It was important to him now that he had decided a course of action. It would be something he could take with him and keep on the inside. He didn't tell anybody his plan while they gathered for the holidays. He did not want to spoil the memory and he did not want to burden his family. They deserved peace.

On January 2nd Mike told his parents that he would be turning himself in soon. He needed them to spend extra time with Myah. They understood and were supportive. He was honest and upfront with them. He gave them his assessment: best case scenario: a few days. Worst case scenario: 18 months.

He outlined his plan to plead not guilty and take it all the way to trial. He decided he was not going to let the system push him against the wall and let them do what they want. Maybe the old Mike was weak-minded and scared like that, but the Mike that was turning himself in understood that submission in the name of his daughter was true strength and that he was ready.

Mike didn't tell his lawyer how he felt. Mike didn't trust him. Mike already knew what he had in his favor, and his case was so old he'd be a fool to cop out. His biggest concern was prepping Myah for the worst.

Over the next few days Mike made sure to spend as much time with Myah as possible. She was getting older, and Mike enjoyed her company. These days, these moments with her gave him strength.

Finally, it was time to tell her. He was sick to his stomach thinking about it.

"Myah, what do you want most in life?" He asked her out of nowhere.

"Nothing. I have enough," she responded smartly. Mike laughed.

"So, there's nothing in the whole wide world that you want?"

She thought about it for a second, her face fixed in taut look of concentration. "A puppy," she answered. Mike laughed.

"Maybe for your birthday, we'll see. What else do you want?"

There was no hesitation this time as she rattled off a list of luxuries: "A vacation with you on a plane, in a hotel, on an island…"

"A few minutes ago you just said there was nothing you wanted, and you had everything you needed!" Mike couldn't stop laughing with her. He was completely blown away by how smart she was.

"Why, are you going somewhere?"

"Yes, I might have to go for job training, and it might be a few weeks, maybe a month." He could feel his throat narrow as a lump formed.

Myah said, "a few weeks, ok, but not a month!" She was tearing up. It was killing Mike. He leaned over and hugged her tight.

"Don't worry, Myah, after the training we will be a

lot happier and I can take you on that vacation, anywhere you want to go." It did little to console her. A few days later, after a lot of searching, Mike found her a puppy exactly like she wanted. She cheered up after that and seemed to forget, if only for a while, that Mike would be leaving.

X

As the date to turn himself in approached, Mike was not nervous at all. He was more anxious to just get it over with. That voice in his head that had seemed so foreign just weeks earlier was now the only voice in his head. It was his consciousness and his conscience. It was maturity.

He would hype himself up every morning in the mirror. His mantra was "if you go into a fight feeling nervous, you've already lost." He was going into this fight calm and precise.

Mike's entire family wanted to come and support him, but he didn't want the court to see his parents cry. He was done with that shit. They weren't going to pump fear into their hearts anymore. He knew it was better if he just faced it alone. He knew he could control himself and did not worry about his emotions in the slightest. With family it was different. The court knew that, and they used it against you. Mike wasn't going to let that happen. This was his burden alone and he would face it alone.

The day finally came. All those years, all those places he had lived, and now his legs had finally stopped running. For the first time in years, he breathed. It was his first real, deep, cleansing breath. He was exhausted, spiritually and physically, but his mind was lucid and sharp.

Mike decided to have a trusted niece with him in the courtroom. She could relay all the pertinent information back to the rest of the family. Mike schooled her on how to behave in the courtroom. No emotions, no fear. Nothing they could use against him. She was cool. She got it.

As they were getting ready to leave, the time had come for Mike's goodbyes. He hugged Myah tighter than he ever had. Mike looked at her face, deep into her eyes and saw Honey. He faltered for just a slight moment but regained his composure before Myah could even notice through her veil of childish tears. Mike kissed her all over and told her everything was going to be all right. And, in his heart, he truly believed it.

The time came for Mike to extricate himself from all the hugs and say goodbye. He and his niece ate a couple of edibles and were on their way.

Mike was calm going into the court building. Once inside the building, he found his attorney in part 19. They sat in the waiting area for about 30 minutes. Mike's name was called, and they made their way into the court room.

Mike took a good look around him. It was real. He took a deep breath to take it all in and they called his indictment number: 05 70xxxx.

New York State vs Michael Lee

The stenographer said the date out loud and there was a pause.

"2005?"

Everyone looked around incredulously, like they couldn't believe what they had just heard. A case from 2005 brought to court in 2021 is not a regular day in court. They did a warrant search to see if he had any other warrants out there that they could hold him on. No warrants were found except for the one they were in court for at that very moment. Mike's parole warrant was no longer valid. He had outrun the parole time limit. It had expired the month before. All that was left was the drug sale warrant from 2005. Luckily, Mike had waived his rights to a grand jury in 2005. With him waiving his rights and pleading not guilty the case was still open.

The court let Mike go on a R.O.R and gave him a court date to return, this time virtually. In that time the district attorney had to provide the evidence report, bring in the arresting officer, basically make the entire case.

Mike looked at his lawyer. "So, I can go now?"

"Yes. You're a free man." Mike turned to his niece, gave her a big hug, and said: "We're out, let's get the fuck out of here.”

XI

The following months were crucial for Mike. He spent his time getting his life together and going back and forth to court. He had a fresh start. He had to learn how to live as a civilian. He had to get ID, a license, a passport, and all the other official things that made people belong to society. It wasn't easy after being a fugitive for 15 years. The passport was the easiest to get, Next, he got his driver's license. It felt weird to live legitimately and to tell people his real name. Lying about his past was easy, he'd had a lot of practice. Mike enjoyed the novelty of these mundane little chores; the things that most people thought of as a "bother" had a lot of significance and he was more than happy to be able to do them. Just being able to use his real name was significant and marked a new chapter in his life. He felt like Honey would finally be proud of him, and that gave him some small comfort.

The weeks passed. Mike's final court date was, of course, set for Friday the 13th. This was it; this was the endgame. He was looking to get it dismissed or AC/DC. His lawyer told him they were going to dismiss the B felony and give Mike disorderly conduct. Mike knew the system. He knew this was a negotiation, nothing more than a game to them. Mike wanted it dismissed, and that's what he told the lawyer.

"They aren't going to do that," the lawyer said. "You have a B felony, which is equivalent to attempted murder. You getting a disorderly conduct is almost unheard of." Mike knew they would never dismiss the charges because that left them vulnerable to a civil suit. So, he did what any rational person would have done. He took the disorderly conduct charge.

And just like that it was over.

Mike called his mom with the good news. Myah got on the phone and said: "You're coming home? Now?"

Mike laughed and said: "Yes ma'am!"

He raced home. All he could think about was sweeping Myah up in his arms and spinning her around and hearing her laugh. When he picked her up and held her up high over his head, he found peace. He had found his life and he wasn't going to do anything to jeopardize it. He owed it to her. He owed it to his parents, his friends. He owed it to Honey. He missed her so much.

XII

Weeks went by and Mike and Myah had settled into

a comfortable routine. Life was almost normal for them. They had lost much, but like the lone survivors of a terrible war, they emerged worn and battered, but still alive and still together. They would forever be the only ones to be able to understand that hollow look in each other's eyes. Only they knew about the missing piece each other carried.

One day, after they had spent the entire day in the city just walking around and talking, Mike felt his life fall into place. He felt right, like everything he was doing was right. There was no fear, no anxiety. There was no restlessness or worry. He had never been so sure about anything in his life. It was a powerful and profound moment for him.

"Daddy, hold my hand. I don't want you to get lost."

Mike laughed. "Don't worry, Myah. You could never lose me."

"Daddy," she said with a serious tone. "I don't want you to be sad anymore. Mommy doesn't want you to be sad, either." She said it matter-of-factly, with the kind of certainty only a child could feel. Looking at her, Mike sensed a maturity beyond her years. In her face he could see the woman she would become. He saw Honey in her face and that made his heart content.

He knew this world, knew its capacity for evil and he knew he would teach his daughter how to navigate that evil and find beauty and happiness wherever she could. He had so much to teach her.

Mike took her small hand in his. It was warm. As they walked back towards the car, the setting sun backlit the Manhattan skyline. Mike paused for a moment to look. It was beautiful. He felt a strong resolve in his heart. He held his head up, scooped his daughter in his arms, and continued walking.

"Are we going home, Daddy?"

"Yes, baby. Let's go home."

THE END